Separation of Church and State

ROBERT L. MADDOX

SEPARATION OF CHURCH AND STATE

Guarantor of Religious Freedom

CROSSROAD • NEW YORK

1987

The Crossroad Publishing Company
370 Lexington Avenue, New York, N.Y. 10017

Printed in the United States of America

Library of Congress Cataloging-in-Publication Data

Maddox, Robert L.
    Separation of church and state: guarantor of religious
freedom / Robert L. Maddox.
        p. cm.
    Bibliography: p.
    ISBN 0-8245-0845-9
    1. Church and state—United States. 2. United States—Church
history. I. Title.
BR516.M253   1987
322'.1'0973—dc

87-15631
CIP

—To my wife and children for their abiding encouragement and confidence

—To the National Advisory Council and the Board of Trustees, Americans United for Separation of Church and State for their commitment to the cause of religious liberty

—To the Staff of Americans United for Separation of Church and State, especially Patricia Thibeaux and Albert Menendez for their unflagging help

Contents

Part One

CRITICAL CONCERNS

CHAPTER ONE

Danger Ahead: Take Alarm

The United States of America was not even dry behind the ears when James Madison cried to his fellow Virginians, "Let us TAKE ALARM at this first experiment on our (religious) liberties." Hard-won freedoms, religious and political, faced imminent danger at the very hands of well-meaning Americans who had risked life and limb to extricate the country from England's stifling grip. His fellow Virginians and ultimately many of his countrymen heard the cry and moved deliberately to ensure religious freedom in a measure never before seen in the history of the world.

Echoing Mr. Madison, I cry to America today, "Take Alarm" lest we fritter away our religious freedom. Polls show a frightening erosion of support for religious freedom and its essential political guarantor, the separation of church and state. All around we encounter a rise in religious intolerance. Sections of the country face the danger of being pulled apart by religious differences.

As the legatees of this grandest of all experiments in religious freedom, Americans today must make new, more profound commitments to religious freedom. We must see, as never before, that liberty of conscience exists as the foundation on which all other freedoms build. If the government or a charismatic religious leader gains the power to coerce, manipulate religious belief and intimidate practices, all our freedoms will crumble. As we Americans race toward the twenty-first century, we must

4 / *Separation of Church and State*

keep burning bright the torch of religious freedom. We must not let anyone or any group destroy the protective wall between church and state. We must pay the price to understand and strengthen the political principle of the separation of church and state.

It is not my business to judge the depth of our national spiritual commitments—a judgment best left to God—but I can say that America is the most actively religious nation in the Western world, with the possible exception of Ireland. In any given week 30 to 40 percent of the American adult population attend some form of religious worship.[1] The American religious enterprise, in its multiple expressions, gives evidence of vigor. A broad, important, if doctrinally imprecise religious tradition pervades American society.

The vitality and pervasiveness of our spiritual life is closely linked to our commitment to religious liberty that has provided the freedom for religious institutions to flourish. We have generally acted with forbearance toward one another's religions, even though some people's faith can look rather bizarre and off the beaten path. As Americans, we insist that all religions, unless demonstrably threatening to life and public well-being, should have equal access to the marketplace of ideas. This spirit of religious free enterprise has encouraged the proliferation of religious groups.

Religious liberty, basic to the way the nation thinks about itself, has endured because church and state have operated separately, with only a minimum of official intrusion into one another's spheres of responsibility. We have insisted that government lean over backward to allow people to gather around their own ideologies and theologies without interference or regulation. We have permitted almost no laws that would inhibit the right of persons to believe and practice as they choose.

The Founding Fathers, reflecting the religious and political realities of their time, enshrined the principle of separation twice in the U.S. Constitution. Article VI of the original text declares: "No religious test shall ever be required as a qualification to any office or public trust under the United States." The religion clauses of the First Amendment affirm: "Congress shall make no law respecting an establishment of religion or prohibiting the free exercise thereof." True, the word "separation" does not appear in the Constitution, but the concept is implicit in the document and is definitely part of the history that produced it.

Our cherished religious liberty, built on a healthy and historic separation of church and state, is under attack. The threat to religious freedom comes from at least four directions: extreme secularists, an intrusive government regulatory apparatus, political and religious ultra-conservatives, and, worst of all, a pervasive public apathy/ignorance. Mix these tangible threats together and the country faces a severe religious liberty crisis.

What do I mean?

A rag-tag army of secularists of undetermined numbers wants to shove religion, which they regard as outmoded and restrictive, to the fringes of national life. These people push to have churches taxed. They throw up irritating roadblocks to the religious enterprise. They seek to deny, undermine, and disregard the reality of America's religious heritage. For the most part, however, contrary to what some hysteria-generating ultra-conservative authors maintain, the secularists are not organized. Secularists are laced through many political and intellectual clusters in national life, but it is a mistake to identify any one group, such as the American Civil Liberties Union, the Humanist Association, or Libertarians, with this minority movement. Militant secularism is more of a mindset than an organization.[2]

Government bureaucracies, at all levels, that do not or will not understand the nature of religious communities make persistent efforts to over-regulate religious activity and, therefore, pose a severe threat to religious liberty. This burgeoning government presence consciously and unconsciously puts unnecessary burdens on faith communities.

The secularists and the government pose serious threats, but today the political forces that present the biggest threat to religious liberty are, ironically, political and religious ultra-conservatives: Catholic, Protestant, Jewish, Democratic and Republican. Shortsighted, right-leaning religious and political leaders seek to manipulate religious energies for their own purposes. Under the banner of religious liberty, leaders from the

Right seek to destroy the protective wall of separation between church and state as they look for ways to use government to enforce their own brand of religion and to garner tax money for their private religious activities. Rather than trust in the inherent force of religion and healthy dialogue to effect moral change, especially individual morality, many work for laws that *impose* their own brand of religiously informed morality on the nation. These people seek to squeeze the American people into a "Stepford Wife" kind of conformity. As the wall crumbles, as separation erodes, church and state suffer—but the church most of all. Leaders from the organizations that lean to the right make scary noises as if they would actually bring religion under some kind of official government umbrella.

But, most of all, our freedoms face the danger of demise, not by decree from legislatures, but rather from apathy and ignorance. In our *not* knowing, we are giving our freedoms away. On one hand, far too many of us take freedom for granted. We never give a second thought to the importance of the separation of church and state. We thus set ourselves up for manipulation by political and religious leaders who are not above moving into the vacuum created by our apathy.

On the other hand, millions of people, religious and non-religious, in a legitimate, but uninformed effort to "do something" about the moral malaise in the country, grasp at strawlike rhetoric that seems to give easy, quick answers to terribly complicated and frustrating problems. Since so many Americans do not know our history, have little grasp of the roots of religious liberty and church/state separation, they deal away this treasure under the sway of glib politicians and preachers. One of the ironies of our present era is that while we talk about wanting less and less government, many actually invite government into their bedrooms and prayer lives. Canny religious and political operatives jump out in front of these concerned but poorly informed millions and lead off in directions dangerous to religious freedom.

In 1785, Patrick Henry introduced a bill into the Virginia Legislature that would levy a general tax for the support of religion. James Madison, a fellow Virginian devoted to religious liberty, rose up in opposition to the venerable Henry and his "assessments" bill. As a major part of his offensive against the bill, Madison wrote a powerful pamphlet called *A Memorial and Remonstrance Against Religious Assessments*. One of Madison's rallying cries in the *Memorial* that turned many in Virginia against the bill was: "Let us take alarm at the first experiment on our liberties."

Today, freedom-loving Americans, religious and non-religious alike, and all across the theological and political landscape, must deflect the political shenanigans that shamefully seek to use legitimate concerns and deep religious convictions for partisan ends. We must filter with extraordinary discernment what we hear from radio and television or read in books, newspapers, and magazines. We should reject self-serving sermons that describe the separation of church and state as a "myth."[3] Let us flee from politicians and preachers who declare that God has told them what to do about the thorny problems of economics, national defense, foreign policy, or space exploration. It's not that God is not interested in such things; he just does not normally convey the answers to such problems in American English. Listen again when candidates for public office declare they speak for the church or the synagogue. No one person can speak *for* religion. Simply because words appear in print, or pour out of a radio or television set, does not mean they are necessarily accurate.

At the same time, we must strengthen our defenses against government and secular incursions into religious life. On the basis of carefully orchestrated, honest political action we can work with, through, and sometimes around government officials to ensure that religious activity gets a fair shake in the town square.

I have confidence in the person in the pew, in the street, in the office, in the home to stem this tide. By paying the price to become and remain informed, we can warn politicians and clergy alike that we will no longer tolerate their *experiment* with our religious liberties. Using the legitimate political avenues at our disposal, we must challenge public figures to deal more responsibly with American history, with the heritage we have in religious liberty, and with the future well-being of both church and state. We must demand that political and religious leaders provide a climate free from government-sponsored sectarian coercion *or* opposition, so that our religious strivings can rise and fall on their own merit. Government at all levels needs the input of compassionate, informed religion, but we do not want to give over the reigns of government to a coalition of religious zealots who arrogantly insist that they alone speak for God.

The American public, not the politicians and preachers, control the elements vital in keeping church and state in balance: votes and money. Through more potent use of the ballot box and more judicious use of the checkbook, we can stop much of this nonsense by politicians and preachers who threaten our liberties. If we pay the price to inform ourselves, we can restore and maintain the essential balance crucial to the relationship between church and state. What's more, contrary to what some TV preachers declare, the twentieth-century U.S. Supreme Court did not invent the separation of church and state. To be sure, a Supreme Court tilted in favor of statism and elitism could destroy religious freedom. Religion, free from support of and management by the state, has existed as a dream and force from colonial days. The political principle of church/state separation, born in colonial days, came largely from men and women of deep religious faith, not secular rationalists.[4] In every way, the future well-being of the nation itself demands that we reinforce religious freedom and the separation of church and state.

I write from a broad but identifiable perspective. I grew up a Southern Baptist in the South. I invested nearly twenty years of my life as a minister in Baptist churches. From my youth I appreciated the freedom we Americans enjoy in all matters, especially in matters of the heart. Under the shadow of such champions of religious liberty as J. M. Dawson, Louie D. Newton, and Glenn Archer, Sr., I gradually came to appreciate that we enjoy religious freedom, in large measure, because of the official, institutional separation of church and state. These giants and others like them taught me that the overarching *spiritual* principle is religious liberty—not a vague, sometimes condescending toleration, but liberty. They went on to say that the time-honored *political* principle for maintaining and undergirding religious liberty is the official separation of church and state.

My commitment to the separation of church and state in no way precludes my active involvement in the political life of the country. Indeed, my religious commitments push me to look carefully at government, to question political leaders, to call for compassion and justice along with such concerns as military capability and law and order. Religious leaders can and should speak to the political life of the nation. To be sure, the manner in which clergy speak and act requires skill and sensitivity, especially in these present days. By taking thought, we can maintain church/state separation and responsible citizenship in a productive, if ambiguous, tension.

I have addressed this book to a general audience, religious and non-religious, lay and clergy, voter and politician. I promise solid research and a fair presentation. The book should not be seen, however, as a dispassionate exercise in scholarship. I am alarmed. I hope to arouse that same emotion in my fellow Americans. I do not call for a holy crusade. Believing that thinking people, not manic crusaders, shape and turn historical tides, I plead for us to put our minds and spirits in gear so that we can wrestle with the problems we face and find the best possible solutions.

CHAPTER TWO

What's a Nice Guy Like You Doing Promoting the Separation of Church and State?

The television-studio crews fidgeted with our microphones and earpieces, told us to look into the camera while we talked, and reminded us that our own voices would be slightly ahead of our images on the monitor before us. Sister Renée Oliver and I, about to debate the pros and cons of the Department of Education's voucher program for parochial and private schools, exchanged pleasantries for a moment. Then the sister, in a quiet voice asked, "What is your background? What did you do before you came to Americans United?"

"I served as a minister in Southern Baptist churches for most of my adult life. I came to this position in the spring of 1984," I explained.

Then the good sister stuck it to me. "I cannot believe that you, a minister, would work for the separation of church and state."

In the seconds before we went on the air, I said, "Sister Renée, my Baptist-preacher ancestors with some of your ancestors in the Roman Catholic Church, along with a hefty sprinkling of other religious people, started the idea of religious liberty through the separation of church and state. A concerned group of ministers, Protestant and Jewish, organized Americans United. I am completely in character as a minister working to maintain church/state separation."

Upon signal, we came on camera and began answering questions by the show's two hosts about the value of the voucher program. After a lively twenty-five minutes, the program ended. Sister Renée and I shook hands and left the studio.

A few days later, however, she called me on the telephone to continue our pre-TV debate conversation. "Don't you believe that your organization has done the country great damage?" she asked. "Don't you believe that you have led to the secularization of this country? You are helping tear down our morals. You are actually hastening the decline of America."

"No, ma'am," I shot back. "America *is* caught in the grips of a rampaging materialism. We have a massive problem of secularism that does threaten to cut us loose from our moral moorings. But the separation of church and state is *not* the villain."

I quickly went on to insist, "Separation of church and state does not mean that moral values and government are separated. It does mean that government is not in the business of legislating religion. Separation has always meant that government cannot attempt to establish one religion over others, or, for that matter, attempt to establish religion, period. It does mean that government, as much as possible, stays out of religious activities.

"Separation means that religion will not take over the engines of government, as has happened in places like Iran. Separation of church and state is the best way yet devised to ensure a free church in a free state. We do not want a state church, nor do we want a church state. The American religious community is the most vital, if diverse, in the Western world precisely because of the healthy wall of separation between church and state."

I assured Sister Renée that one could be fully committed to morality and transcendent values and still insist that we avoid the dangers of a state church or a church state. Maybe she felt better after we talked. We both agreed that we would never agree on certain issues of the present church/state conflict but that we should find ways to work together for the values on which we were able to agree.

I wish that Sister Renée were the only American confused about the idea of the separation of church and state. She's not. Administration officials, some television evangelists, and people in the street have settled on a distorted notion of religious liberty through the separation of church and state. The confusion offers opportunity for grave mischief. People in high places capitalize on the climate of confusion and willingly succumb to the temptation to manipulate emotions and fears for their own gain. Unfortunately, history bleeds with stories that show what happens when unscrupulous persons use religious emotions for their own ends. Corrupting the language of religious liberty, some leaders would actually undercut our freedom to worship by pushing the state to support a hybrid brand of Judeo-Christian religion as the official faith of the nation.

Why the conscious or unconscious distortion?

Many Americans look at our rambunctious country with its constantly changing mores and sigh, "If only we could go back to simpler days. We used to pray in school. We read the Bible. We did not have drugs. People stayed married." To these folks, with their eyeshades of nostalgia, America used to be more stable. Ozzie and Harriett lived down the tree-lined street. Around the corner you could find Fibber McGee and Molly, with only their cluttered hall closet to worry about. The Great Gildersleeve made us laugh.

Along come well-meaning leaders who suggest that today's problems can be linked to the demise of school prayer and required Bible reading. Reverend Jones no longer comes for his weekly visit to the elementary school to tell Bible stories. And, what's more, they don't have band concerts in the city park on the Fourth of July anymore, either. The culprit, we are told, is the separation of church and state. So, the way to restore America is to do away with the wall of separation between church and state.

Let a few TV preachers and a few highly placed politicians come down on church/state separation and, in a flash, an army of tag-alongs join in saying, "Right. Let's abandon the *modern* heresy of the separation of church and state. Let's rewrite the U.S. Constitution to make sure that we give proper allegiance to religion."

Extreme?

Not at all. Listen to some of the politically oriented preachers and some of the religiously oriented politicians and you will find out what I am talking about.

By now, some readers may be screaming, "Wait just a minute!

America needs all the religion it can get. Religion makes people behave and we certainly do need for Americans to calm down and act right."

Granted. America does need all the just and compassionate religious input it can get. No mistake. But the government must not, indeed cannot, by its nature be the evangelist. In a constitutional democracy like ours, government, in whatever form, has no role in *promoting* religion. To be sure, government must do its best to avoid interfering with the free exercise of religion. By the same token, the religious community must not look to government to do its work for it. Government and religion can be friends, neighbors, but they must not try to share the same house and never, never should they get married.

In these next pages I want to celebrate America's great gift to itself: religious liberty.

Let's take a poll. Everyone in favor of religious liberty, raise your hand. There, see. Every hand shot up.

Now, let's ask: How do we *maintain* religious liberty for 235 million Americans, many of whom are scattered into something like three thousand religious groups?[1] What happens when the competing interests and doctrines of these groups begin to bump into each other? What happens when a majority faith in your town tries to run roughshod over a minority religion? And what happens when a scrappy minority sect begins to push and shove against the majority? For instance, how do we best serve the cause of religious liberty when a small congregation of Jehovah's Witnesses in a South Georgia town questions patriotic and religious practices of the community's WASP majority? Trouble in the camp? You're right.

A few days before I made a speech to a Baptist gathering, the U.S. Park Service had decided to allow a private group to place a Nativity Scene on the Ellipse in Washington as part of the Christmas decorations. Jewish groups, especially, objected to the Park Service's decision to allow a religious symbol on public property. I tried to explain the complexities of such a simple looking act by the U.S. government to my Baptist audience. Most of the congregation seemed to understand.

After the service, however, a man walked up and said, "We Christians are in the majority in this country. We can do what we want to. If the Jews and other groups don't like it, let 'em leave. We have power. Let's use it."

Is that the way we want to operate in this country?

Let's talk about it.

CHAPTER THREE

Flash Points

In my work I appear on numerous radio and television talk shows. If you want to know what a large segment of the American people think, just tune in to some of those programs, especially radio call-in shows.

The subject of religion and politics always lights up the station's switchboard. I have done as much as three hours at a time, with never a lull in the calls. If I kept score, my hunch is that more callers are against, or ar least confused about, the meaning of the separation of church and state. Explain as I do that church/state separation does not mean a "Godless" nation, many callers never get the message.

One comment crops up time and again: "America is a Christian nation. Christians, therefore, should call the political and religious shots."

Several times, the callers have said something like, "Since this is a Christian nation, we ought to *make* everyone be a Christian. If they don't want to be Christians, let them go someplace else."

What about the oft-repeated assertion that: America was created as a Christian nation? Callers point to all the references to religion in the history surrounding the settlement in America. Who among us has not misted up at the thought of the first Thanksgiving, of George Washington kneeling in the snow at Valley Forge, references to God in the Declaration of Independence, Franklin's plea for prayer during the 1787 Constitutional Convention, and the many other religious references in the opening days of the nation?

What about political activism by religious groups? The lines between religious concern and political activism can get fuzzy, indeed. Government and religion at all levels struggle to address the problem of religious involvement in politics. The jury is still out on this question.

For instance:

A few years ago, the State of Tennessee enacted a campaign disclosure law[1] designed to monitor contributions to political campaigns. Under the law, groups who contribute to political campaigns must register as political action committees and provide certain campaign disclosure records. The law passed the state legislature with little opposition. The legislative history of the passage of the law makes no mention of churches coming under the regulation.

In the summer of 1985, a group of churches—Baptist, Church of Christ, Pentecostal and Methodist—in Jackson, Tennessee, decided to oppose a local liquor-by-the-drink referendum. Some of the churches took out ads in the newspaper. Others offered to drive voters to the polls. Some put small amounts of money into a political action committee that had formed to oppose the referendum. The "drys" won, meaning that Jackson would continue its ban on liquor-by-the-drink in restaurants, hotels, etc.

Someone in the town called the state Attorney General's office and asked for an investigation into the churches' activities. The Attorney General's office checked out the situation in Jackson and ruled that the participating churches came under the campaign disclosure law and would have to register as political action committees because of their activity in the referendum. The churches refused, and have now challenged the constitutionality of the Tennessee law, at least as the Attorney General applied it to the churches.

What about that?

In the heat of political campaigns, it looks as if some churches, black and white, are turning themselves into ward headquarters for political candidates with whom they agree. These churches allegedly conduct voter registration, not just to get their people signed up to vote as a matter of civic duty, but they get them registered with instructions to vote for certain candidates.

When one potential presidential candidate, running as a born-again, garnered a few delegates in the earliest part of a selection process, he put out a fund-raising letter declaring, "The Christians have won!!"

What about that?

An abortion-rights group sued the Internal Revenue Service, seeking to force the government agency to lift the tax-exempt status of Roman Catholic churches and even the national organization of Catholic bishops because of the church's involvement in anti-abortion politics. The abortion rights group says the bishops and their congregations openly promote candidates who agree with their own view of abortion.

One municipality came down hard on a group of churches that provided shelter for the homeless on cold nights. The zoning board of the city claimed the churches had converted themselves into hotels, thus violating zoning ordinances, by providing bed and board to poor people. "Besides," one rather zealous city official said, "it's not the job of the churches to provide shelter. Government ought to do that."

In one of his State of the Union addresses, President Reagan lamented, "God has been expelled from the public schools"; and: "Congress can open its sessions with prayer, but boys and girls in public schools cannot." Many in the packed chamber of the House of Representatives and around the country cheered.

TV preachers tell the horror story of a schoolgirl who bowed her head at lunchtime in the cafeteria to offer grace silently for her food, whereupon Simon Legree, in the form of the principal, interrupted her with the warning, "Praying in school, even silently, violates the separation of church and state. You cannot do *that* here."

Teenagers who chose not to participate in the weekly, pre-school Bible study at their high school in Little Axe, Oklahoma had to wait outside in the cold until the opening bell rang. Their classmates jeered and the teacher-leader of the Bible study scowled at the students because they did not attend the religious exercise. The house of one of the dissenting families was mysteriously destroyed by fire. One of the dissenting mothers was attacked on the school parking lot by an irrational supporter of the prayer group.[2]

Some public school teachers received a scolding because they gathered in a corner of the public school during lunch break for an informal reading of the Bible and prayer time.[3]

Fundamentalist preachers pray that God will remove certain Supreme Court justices, "in any appropriate manner," so that the way can be cleared to again allow God back on the public high school campus. One such preacher at the Baptist Temple in Los Angeles even prayed for the death of Justice William Brennan of the High Court.[4]

Besides, what's wrong with a little school prayer, anyway?

What kind of religious activity can take place on public school campuses? Has the U.S. Supreme Court kicked God out of public education? On one of my talk shows, a caller lamented, "The young Communists can meet on the high school campus but the young Christians cannot. Where's religious liberty in that, huh?" Have the secular humanists taken over the teaching profession?

Some state legislatures have tried to require the teaching of "creation science" alongside the study of evolution. The lawmakers do not seek to outlaw the teaching of evolution. They simply want equal time given, not to the Bible, but to "creation science" as that unique academic discipline is called by its proponents.

In the summer of 1985, the U.S. Supreme Court, in three related cases, said it violated the U.S. Constitution to use tax money to send public school teachers onto the premises of religious schools. These particular cases involved public school teachers going to parochial schools for the purpose of providing remedial education. According to the Supreme Court, remedial education can occur for all students—public or parochial—at public expense, but public school teachers going onto church property violates the Establishment clause of the First Amendment.

Church/state separationists hailed the decision. Members of the sitting Adminstration decried the ruling as "wrong-headed, bizarre, out of step with the Founding Fathers."

Should the state provide tax money for parochial schools in the form of grants, tuition tax credits, redeemable vouchers, free food, transportation, extra teachers?

What about the argument by parents with children in religious schools who say the tax laws punish them because they choose not to use the public schools. These parents decry the monopoly that public schools have on the education of our youth.

Bishops take to the political hustings to promote a referendum that would amend a state's constitution to allow public funding of private, parochial schools. Another Catholic leader warns the bishops to be wary of taking public money lest they ultimately lose control of the religious thrust of the very schools they seek to save with tax money.

When President Harry Truman talked about appointing a U.S. ambassador to the Holy See of the Roman Catholic Church at the Vatican, his own pastor denounced the idea from the pulpit. Such a hue and cry went up around the country that General Mark Clark, the nominee, asked that his name be withdrawn. The President "harrumphed," dropped the idea, and probably told Bess where he wished most of those preachers would go. He never attended that church again, either.

In an unheralded move in the fall of 1983, the U.S. Senate quietly passed legislation that cleared the way for President Reagan to appoint an ambassador to the Holy See and Pope John Paul II. A few religious leaders raised a cry but failed to muster the troops. The President nominated. The Senate confirmed. Religious leaders seriously protested, but the job was done. Jerry Falwell raised an eyebrow at his favorite president over the appointment, but Billy Graham said, "It's no big deal." So now we have an ambassador to the Vatican.

The Supreme Court said that the city of Pawtucket, Rhode Island—the state that saw the birth of religious freedom in America—could use tax money to put up a Nativity Scene in a public park during Christmas shopping days. A narrow 5-to-4 majority of the U.S. Supreme Court said the city's action was constitutional because the Nativity Scene had simply become part of the American Christmas celebration like Santa Claus and Rudolph. The dissenting justices lamented the decision, saying, "If the Nativity Scene is anything at all, it is a deeply religious symbol." "Liberal" preachers stuck with the dissenting opinion while "fundamentalist" preachers lauded the majority decision. Makes you wonder who's for Jesus and who's for Santa Claus.

What about religious activity on public property?

When the Pope came to the United States in 1979, the city of Philadelphia paid for a worship center on which John Paul II celebrated Mass. When this was challenged in court, the judge said the city violated the U.S. Constitution's ban on establishing a religion. The Philadelphia Catholic diocese had to come up with money to pay for the worship stand. By contrast, the diocese of Washington secured permission to use the Washington Mall for the Pope's mass, but the bishop had the foresight to pay for the worship center from church funds. No problem.

About three years after going to work in a Florida jewelry store, an employee joined the Seventh-day Adventist Church. Her religious conviction prevented her working on Saturdays. At first her employers allowed her to take Saturday off, provided she would work on Sundays. She readily agreed to their plan. Then they changed their minds and forced her either to work some on Saturdays or resign. The State of Florida would not give her unemployment compensation when she filed for losing her job because of religious reasons. The state said the fact that she had changed her religion after going to work at the store cost her her rights to the compensation. What about that?

The Church of Jesus Christ of Latter-day Saints, the Mormon Church, owns a public gymnasium in Salt Lake City, Utah. The facility is open to the public, is not central to the ministry of any congregation in Salt Lake, and is generally run like a business. Many years ago, the managers of the gymnasium employed a gentleman, a Mormon, one who was not particularly active in the church, to run the facility. At some point, the church overseers of the gym decided that all employees should be tithe-paying members of the church. When the director of the gym refused to comply with the managers' demands, they fired him. He sued, charging discrimination. The church countered by saying it had the right to hire whom it wanted to because of its nature as a church.

Who's right and who's wrong? The Supreme Court will have to decide.

I could go on. You can readily see that the wall of separation between church and state is anything but clearly marked. It is high and low, wide and narrow, solid and quite porous, straight and zigzagged.

Church/state cases have become part of the clog in the state and federal judicial pipeline. At this writing, the Christian Legal Society estimates that approximately 220 church/state cases growing out of honest disputes over the best way for church and state to relate are in the judicial pipeline.[5]

Why the confusion? Why so many cases?

Some observers say the multiplication of court cases is a sign of the decay of American religion, a sign of secular humanism. If only the Supreme Court would leave religion alone, everything would be fine.

I disagree.

The number of cases, the presence of conflict, is a sign of vitality. We do have a religious community that takes its issues seriously. When negotiation fails, Americans turn to the courts, even in matters of religion. If religious people did not care what happened, they would simply roll over and play dead when challenged.

Do we abandon a fundamental principle because of confusion? Not at all. The confusion points to the need for the principle. If we did not have the First Amendment, it would have to be created. My travels to other countries for religious liberty conferences points up two facts: Confusion over the relationship between church and state exists in all free societies; our First Amendment provides the fairest way to deal with church/state problems.

It is patent nonsense to lay our problems at the door of an activist court system. Courts do not generate cases. *People* bring lawsuits to the courts. Courts do not go out and find lawsuits. They simply decide between disputing parties who show up before the bench.

I celebrate American religious diversity and energy. By nature, I do not like conflict. I wish we could settle our differences without resorting to expensive, time-consuming court battles. But at least we settle our disputes with words and not bullets, as they do in some parts of the world when religious people get crossed up. I'll take our system, with all its flaws, over any other that I have encountered so far.

Part Two

HISTORICAL PERSPECTIVE

CHAPTER FOUR

Start in the Middle of the Story

No one likes to come into the theater in the middle of the story. In trying to understand the development of religious liberty in America, however, I find such a mid-entry a helpful place to begin.

Thomas Jefferson's statement about the "*wall* of separation between church and state" represents the sum total of what many people know about the subject. Indeed, many people express surprise to learn that the "wall of separation" is not constitutional language but rather Jefferson's shorthand way of interpreting the First Amendment.

As we begin to understand where this whole church/state separation idea originated, we do well to begin with Jefferson, though the story does not really begin with him. In a sense, his "wall" idea is the gathering place, the focal point, the Continental Divide, if you please, for this entire discussion. Before the adoption of the religious-freedom clauses of the First Amendment and the "wall" interpretation Jefferson placed on it, the movement of American history was toward the concept of the separation of church and state. After the First Amendment/"wall" concept, church/state relations are measured, governed, and understood by this Jeffersonian idea. So, let's begin with Jefferson and his wall.

The Baptists of Connecticut, exuberantly practicing their faith in the twenty-five-year-old United States in the Year of Our

Roger Williams
~163—

Lord 1801 had a strong appreciation for President Thomas Jefferson. In spite of the charge of "atheist" hurled at Jefferson by some religious Americans, especially New England Congregationalists, many Baptists had supported his election. The Baptists of Connecticut and the other states in the Union enjoyed unprecedented freedom, thanks in large part to the tall, angular Virginian presently occupying the, as yet, unfinished White House in Washington City. The Baptists wholeheartedly endorsed the President's conviction that religion ought to stand on its own without the support or interference of the government.

But the Baptists could not fully understand their president either. This reflective, sensitive, in his own way religious man, now the third President of the United States, steadfastly refused to proclaim days of fasting and prayer as his predecessors, Washington and Adams, had done.

Probably at a meeting of the Baptist Association in Danbury, Connecticut, some of the key leaders of the association puzzled over Mr. Jefferson's reluctance to call the nation to prayer. Having attended dozens of those Baptist meetings in my own time, and being fully persuaded that we Baptists have not changed all that much across two centuries, I can just imagine the conversation that must have taken place.

One good brother would have said, "I like the President, but maybe some of the people were right about him. Maybe he is an atheist."

Another would have said, "My nephew has a friend who grew up in the next county to Jefferson's down in Virginia. I get the word that his religion is definitely strange."

"I think we ought to have a press conference and question the President's convictions. We certainly ought not to have an atheist for President," yet another vigorous, quick-draw reverend could have popped up.

Then, at the right moment, perhaps, a quiet voice rose over the din. "Gentleman, I suggest we write to the President and ask him why he does not issue prayer proclamations. We could waste a lot of the Lord's time sitting around here speculating. As good a friend as he is to us Baptists, it would be a shame and the height of ingratitude for us to denounce him in the press—certainly without first giving him a chance to speak for himself. I propose that we draft a letter to the President. Wish him a Happy New Year. In the letter, ask him why he hesitates to call the nation to prayer."

Before the historians object to my rendering, I hasten to say I have found no historic record of the actual meeting of Danbury Baptists. Even after considerable research, I have not been able to produce the actual content of the letter the Baptists of Danbury wrote to Mr. Jefferson. We do know that he wrote to the Connecticut Baptists. We have reason to believe the Baptists' letter wished Mr. Jefferson well in the new year, 1802, and that the letter asked why he would not follow in his predecessors' footsteps by issuing the proclamations.[1]

With that bit of docu-drama, let's at least sample the history that saw the birth of religious liberty in America. I tried every way possible to avoid a history lesson but had to give in. Understanding of today's situation demands a quick but careful look at the past.

Please stay with me for this backward look. To help us get this history lesson more clearly in mind, I want us to move in rather awkward directions. In this chapter, as I have said, I want us to focus on Jefferson and his "wall" as well as get a feeling for what others of our Founders said and felt about religious freedom.

Then, I want to walk backward before going forward. In the next chapter, we will go back even further to examine the roots of religious liberty in the Middle Ages. Next, we will come to the New World, to colonial, pre-Revolutionary America. Then, if you please, let's examine the creation of the U.S. Constitution and the First Amendment before we begin to proceed in a more linear historical manner.

Let me do that again, in outline form:

Jefferson's "wall," the middle of the story.

The leap way back to the Middle Ages.

Colonial America.

The formation of the Constitution and the First
Amendment.

Then, the leap over Jefferson's "wall" to the nineteenth century,

—as we move into modern times.

Thomas Jefferson, our third president, planted in the nation's
consciousness the phrase, "the *wall* of separation between church
and state." Mr. Jefferson did not invent the phrase.

Roger Williams (1603–1683), the Quaker-turned-Baptist-
turned-Seeker, and the founder of Rhode Island, may have
first uttered the phrase when he talked about the "hedge or
wall of separation between the garden of the church and the
wilderness of the world."[2] Thanks to Roger Williams and other
colonial religious leaders, the idea that church and state ought
to function in separate spheres had a growing, if uneven, acceptance in America. The road from religious intolerance in
the earliest days of colonial America to the brilliance of religious
liberty in the constitutional era runs anything but straight. It is
clear, however, that by the time of the American Revolution a
broad, but certainly not unanimous, consensus had emerged
that church and state should function separately. All that notwithstanding, history gives Mr. Jefferson most of the credit for
the phrase that has come to describe the American understanding of the way church and state should best relate.

The President took the occasion of the Baptist letter to describe carefully his views on church and state. Apparently in
order to determine the constitutionality of his reply before post-
ing it, Mr. Jefferson consulted with Levi Lincoln, his attorney
general, seeking Mr. Lincoln's comments on the letter to the
Baptist leaders. In the cover letter to the Attorney General,
Jefferson said, "I know it [the response] will give great offence
to the New England clergy; but the advocate of religious freedom is to expect neither peace nor forgiveness from them."[3]

In a long but magnificent sentence, Thomas Jefferson wrote:
"Believing with you that religion is a matter which lies solely
between man and his God, that he owes account to none other
for his faith or his worship, that the legislative powers of gov-

ernment reach actions only, and not opinions, I contemplate with sovereign reverence that the act of the whole American people which declared that their legislature should 'make no law respecting an establishment of religion, or prohibiting the free exercise thereof,' thus building a *wall* of separation between Church and State."[4]

There, you have the phrase.

Now, let's examine it for just a few minutes. As we stand in awe before Mr. Jefferson's statement and its diamond-like facets, we have to ask some basic questions. Why did Jefferson make the statement? What did the phrase mean to the President? What part, if any, did his views on church and state play in the formation of the U.S. Constitution and the Bill of Rights?

Given Mr. Jefferson's careful attention to detail, we can assume he did not make the statement lightly, or without regard to the historical setting out of which the phrase came.

President Thomas Jefferson clearly broke with his predecessors, Messrs. Washington and Adams, by refusing to issue proclamations calling for days of prayer and thanksgiving. Was he an atheist? Was he asking the nation to forsake its religious roots? No, on both counts. He would not issue such proclamations because he felt he did not have the constitutional authority to lead the people in acts of religious worship. Furthermore, as the author of the Virginia Statute on Religious Freedom and one of the major sources of the ideas and philosophy behind the Religion Clause of the First Amendment, Mr. Jefferson's strong view of the separation of church and state threw up philosophical roadblocks in his own mind that persuaded him not to take on the role of priest and pastor.[5]

Jefferson had grown up in Virginia as a member of the officially established Anglican Church. Religion had been important to the rangy Virginian. He never entertained an idea about being *against* religion. As years went by, he did structure his own religious attitudes, becoming something of a Unitarian/Deist in his theology. But faith, belief in God and immortality, and service to his fellow human beings remained part of his world view.[6]

In pre-Revolutionary Virginia, the Church of England enjoyed official support by the government. All the citizens of the colony paid taxes for the support of the Anglican Church. From time to time, preachers of non-established churches received penalties, even prison terms, for preaching without a proper license from the government. Magistrates did not hesitate to get involved in disputes over religion. Public officials enforced not only standards of morality, they made decisions involving strictly religious matters.

Wide-ranging reading, including the works of John Locke, the influence of men like fellow Virginian George Mason, the particular cultural streams including the Enlightenment from which Jefferson drank—linked with his own sensitive spirit— combined to push Jefferson, from his earliest days as a public servant, to contemplate religious liberty and the separation of church and state.

Jefferson's thinking and writing took on concrete reality when his Virginia Statute on Religious Liberty, passed by the legislature in 1786 during his tenure as Ambassador to France, disestablished the Anglican Church in Virginia. The Virginia statute served as a helpful model to other states as they formed constitutions that provided for religious liberty and the separation of church and state. Even more to the point, Jefferson's writings and thinking profoundly influenced James Madison, the chief architect of the U.S. Constitution and the Bill of Rights. Thus, Jefferson's views on the separation of church and state both reflected and more clearly refined the mood of the new country's people and their lawmakers on the issue of the relationship between church and state.

What did the "wall" mean to Thomas Jefferson? The statement as a whole reflects Jefferson's understanding of religion, namely that one's religion was intensely personal and individualistic. Religion is "solely" a matter for a man and his God. The fact that the country had ratified the Bill of Rights persuaded Jefferson that the American people agreed with his understanding of religious freedom and the separation of church and state.

Jefferson's use of the "wall" described his profound belief that government should not interfere with the inalienable right of a person freely to practice his or her religion. Government was totally incompetent to make religious pronouncements, especially in matters of individual faith.

Furthermore, Jefferson reflected the pervasive but, again, not universal belief that gave birth to the Religion Clauses of the First Amendment; namely, that religion should be maintained and supported voluntarily. Government attempts to organize and regulate support for religion involved a seizure of power, a violation of soul liberty, and should not happen in the United States.[7]

Of course, not everyone shared the views espoused by Jefferson; Patrick Henry, for instance. Some seventeen years before Jefferson's Baptist letter, the eloquent, super-patriot Mr. Henry stated, through a bill he introduced into the Virginia legislature, that the state should take a definite hand in supporting religion by taxing all citizens for the support of "teachers of religion"— meaning, primarily—clergy in the Episcopal Church. Those citizens who did not belong to the Episcopal Church could designate the preachers to whom their taxes would go: sort of an eighteenth-century version of educational vouchers.

Many in the Virginia legislature who could, as yet, hardly conceive of the idea of "no establishment of religion" supported Henry's efforts. Even George Washington, still in the process at that time of refining his views on church and state, gave some support to the assessments bill.[8] Why not? The tax levy would provide for all clergy. The legislature was not establishing any one church. Besides, cohesive, homogenized, stable religion was good for the state. What was more, several of their sister states had various forms of assessments bills designed to support clergy through public taxes.

James Madison, then in his early thirties, gained his political wings in the legislative battle to thwart the tax for religion. Patrick Henry enjoyed such unquestioned support in the legislature that Madison had to resort to the parliamentary move of having the measure tabled. During a legislative recess, Madison and his cohorts hurried around and got Henry elected Governor of Virginia, a position that, under Virginia's post-Revolutionary constitution, neutralized his efforts to push through the assessments bill. Madison then wrote his great defense of religious liberty, *A Memorial and Remonstrance,* which provided both banner and language for those who opposed the proposed legislation.

During the months in which the assessments bill lay on the table, many people in the state rallied with Madison against it, especially the Baptists and Presbyterians, thus enabling opponents to get it sidetracked. Interestingly enough, the demise of the assessments bill occurred because liberals like Madison and conservatives like the Baptists and Presbyterians joined forces to correct a constitutional wrong before it got started. If you please, the thunder of religious fervor on the right and the ice water of reason on the left combined to stop the assessments bill.[9]

The defeat of Henry's bill set the stage for passage of Jefferson's Statute on Religious Freedom in 1786, which in turn helped prepare the country for the First Amendment in 1791.

Bottom line: The people of Virginia began to say they did not want the government funding religion.[10]

Was this anti-clericalism rearing its ugly head? Had Virginia turned against religion? Could it be that Virginia's political leaders had become secular humanists? No, on all counts. The advocates of complete religious liberty who opposed Patrick Henry's bill made the case that legitimate religion stood on its own and did not need the support of the state.

Well, we can understand the separationist ideas of Jefferson and the accommodationist views of Patrick Henry. What about the views of other Founding Fathers on the role of the state in promoting and encouraging religion? As one would suspect, the attitudes of the Founding Fathers toward religion and religious freedom were varied, reflecting an increasingly diverse country.

Indeed, one of the important reasons for America's commitment to religious freedom was this very diversity.[11] Though Protestant Christianity was the prevailing *flavor* of American religion, Americans expressed their faith through several competing denominations: Anglican, Congregational, Quaker, Baptist, Presbyterian, Reformed, Moravian, Mennonite, Lutheran, and Methodist. And within these large clusters the impact of geography and church leadership further pulled the people into subgroups. For instance, the Baptists in Virginia held somewhat different views on church doctrine than did their brothers and sisters in New England. Outside the Protestant fold a few Roman Catholics and Jews struggled for a place.

So, as the leaders began to create the nation and its institutions, they brought religious as well as political differences to the bargaining tables.

Before we talk, however, about differences, we do well to focus on the points of agreement that bound the Founders together. Many of them held deep religious convictions, though some, like Jefferson and Franklin, thought and lived outside orthodox lines. Our leaders had a keen appreciation for the spiritual and religious impulses of the American people. They understood a person's religious feelings to be so intensely personal that the state should not interfere at all. Nearly all had a rather utilitarian thread running through their theology that led them to recognize the power of religion to stabilize and strengthen individuals and the country as a whole.

These—by and large young—men who shaped the nation determined to avoid authoritarianism in government and religion. They did not want an anti-liberty, anti-religion state— nor a religious monopoly.[12]

But, having crystallized their major points of agreement, we need to understand and admit, for the record, that our Founding Fathers also enjoyed something less than unanimity on the precise way church and state should relate.

If Thomas Jefferson and James Madison had their heads together on religious liberty and church/state separation, their colleagues were scattered along the road somewhere behind them— but generally headed in the Jeffersonian/Madisonian direction. Mason, Jefferson, and Madison had cogitated on religious-liberty issues for years, but many Americans even in key places of leadership had not thought along those lines, at least not as carefully as had the three Virginians. The idea of complete religious liberty and its corollary, the separation of church and state, had, as we have seen, been incubating for decades along with the belief in the right and ability of a people to govern themselves without a king and without an official church to prop up the king.[13] But such radical notions took some getting used to.

In today's struggle to map out church/state relations we make regular reference to the Founding Fathers. As with the Bible, one can "prove" almost any point by lifting quotes out of context. In the course of long public careers and voluminous correspondence and writings, our early leaders made a wide variety of statements on religion and religious freedom. Sometimes they made apparently contradictory statements. Over a period of years they changed their minds, sometimes advancing, sometimes retreating. To get at what was happening as we try to arrive at clearer guidelines for today, we have to attempt to put together the larger picture. We have to look at what the Founders said not only in a given situation but what they said in the sweep of creating the new nation. Along with Thomas Jefferson, the father of religious liberty in America, let's look at Benjamin Franklin, George Washington, James Madison, and John Adams.

Benjamin Franklin's religious roots reached into the Presbyterian Church but, from the time he could think, he thought for himself. At twenty-two, in his *Articles of Belief and Acts of Religion,* he set forth his philosophy of life and faith. He intended to avoid "censure." He would have "evenness of mind." In the thick of constitutional debate during the momentous summer of 1787, he gave a clue about his political and religious openness when he said, "Our different sentiments on almost every question is . . . proof of the imperfection of human understanding"—thus precluding the establishment of one religion over another.

Yet this man whose lack of theological orthodoxy let him embrace and glean what he regarded the best from all the "sects" pleaded, unsuccessfully, for daily prayers to be offered by Philadelphia's ministers before the delegates of the 1787 constitutional convention. Prayer, for Franklin, was not a clever way to bring the Deity over to his way of thinking; rather, prayer gathered up individuals and groups so they could resonate with a force beyond themselves. Anything but traditional in his views, Franklin nonetheless operated from a world view laced through with religion.

Naturally, his own expansive view of religion would persuade him to religious freedom. We have no record that Mr. Franklin specifically used the phrase "separation of church and state", but in one of his many discourses history records him as saying, "When a religion is good, I conceive it will support itself; and when it does not support itself, and God does not take care to support it so that its professors are obliged to call for help of the civil power, 'tis a sign, I apprehend, of its being a bad one."[14]

Franklin died a year before the Bill of Rights was adopted, but one can imagine him leaning over the battlements of heaven cheering his fellow Pennsylvanians on toward ratification.

George Washington epitomizes the Founding Father whose life and statements can be used to prove just about any point. Some biographers insist he was not a believer, that he merely used religion to keep soldiers and citizens in line. Others mythologize the man, bestowing on him a sort of evangelical sainthood. Somewhere in the middle of that conflicting rhetoric is the real man. One scans his statements and correspondence dealing with matters of religion, and Washington's skill as a politician comes through. Probably everyone with whom he communicated claimed him as his own.

As a well-born Virginian, he naturally received religious instruction as an Episcopalian. The death of his father when George was still a youngster, the way he quickly took to the life outdoors, his early introduction into military life, the undeniable leadership qualities he possessed so abundantly—all this pushed him away from standard participation in the life of a local parish. All of his life, however, he gave evidence of religious faith. What's more, he reflected the country's growing attitude toward religious toleration; then, on to freedom. Not a philosopher, he did not clearly enunciate his views, but he certainly practiced and advocated religious freedom.

In a 1775 letter to General Benedict Arnold, Washington insisted, "While we are contending for our own liberty, we should be very cautious of violating the rights of conscience in others . . ."[15]

To a church in Baltimore, Washington wrote:

> We have abundant reason to rejoice that in this Land the light of truth and reason has triumphed over the power of bigotry and superstition, and that every person may here worship God according to the dictates of his own heart. In this enlightened Age and in this land of equal liberty it is our boast that a man's religious tenets will not forfeit the protection of the laws, nor deprive him of the right of attaining and holding the highest offices that are known in the United States.[16]

He probably pondered little about the separation of church and state. Church/state separation as enunciated by Jefferson and Madison was not a major part of his thinking. For instance, with no thought at all about the problems of government's funding religion, he used chaplains in the army—a practice that has continued.

In defending the lack of religious language in the new U.S. Constitution, Washington wrote to a group of church leaders saying:

> I am persuaded, you will permit me to observe, that the path of true piety is so plain as to require but little political direction . . . To the guidance of the ministers of the gospel the important object is, perhaps, more properly committed. It will be your care to instruct the ignorant, and to reclaim the devious, and, in the progress of morality and science, to which our government will give every furtherance, we may confidently expect the advancement of true religion, and the completion of our happiness.[17]

To a Hebrew congregation President Washington wrote, "For happily the Government of the United States, which gives bigotry no sanction, to persecution no assistance, requires only that they who live under its protection should demean themselves as good citizens, in giving it on all occasions their effectual support."[18]

To sum up Washington's views it is clear that he had a strong religious bent. He believed that God, Providence, the Author of the Universe, etc., had control of the affairs of men and nations. Throughout his life he never wavered on the importance of religious liberty. Religion and morality were essential to the well-being of the country. Religious instruction was the primary responsibility of clergy. Government, while needing the underpinning of "true religion," should get only minimally involved in the promotion of religion.

If George Washington gathered everyone up by his religious pronouncements, John Adams scattered them. John Adams possessed a deep religious faith, but his irascible personality, his Yankee honesty, kept religious people of all points of view mad at him.

He could sing the praises of Christianity: "Christianity is the brightness of the glory and the express portrait of the character of the eternal . . . the first good, the first first, the first fair."[19] He could also explode: "Ever since the Reformation, when or where has existed a Protestant or dissenting sect who could tolerate A Free Inquiry? . . . The most yahooish brutality is patiently endured, countenanced, propagated, and applauded." Collide with a "dogma of sect" and you will "find you have a disturbed a nest, and the hornets will swarm about your legs and hands and fly into your face and eyes."[20] Though he quarreled with organized religion, he was a faithful churchman, a devoted Unitarian. Perhaps because he felt so strongly about religion, he could criticize people of religion who not did measure up to their own avowed standards.

In keeping with many of the Founders—indeed, setting the pace, no doubt—John Adams championed "liberty of conscience." In 1782 he wrote: ". . . I am an enemy of every appearance of restraint in a matter so delicate and sacred as the liberty of conscience."[21] To Richard Price, in 1785, he wrote: "I am happy to find myself perfectly agreed with you, that we should begin by setting conscience free. When all men of all religions consistent with morals and property, shall enjoy equal liberty . . . and when government shall be considered as having in it nothing more mysterious or divine than other arts or sciences, we may expect that improvements will be made in the human character and the state of society."[22]

Adams, like his contemporaries, valued religion for itself and also for its benefits to society. He did not speak precisely to the relationship of government and religion. His sentiments, as gleaned from his writings, lay with freedom of religion. He did lampoon established religions, which probably made many of his fellow citizens in Massachusetts uncomfortable because the state still regarded Congregationalism as the official church.

Though Adams evidently felt no compulsion to develop a theory of church and state, his commitments were certainly in the direction of non-interference by government in a person's religious life, and he would certainly have urged the churches to fight their own moral and spiritual battles without asking government for help. His libertarian views had a particularly sharp cutting edge in his native state because of Massachusetts' lingering affection for an established church.

By any measure, James Madison goes down in American history as the chief engineer of the constitutional era and has earned the title "Father of the Constitution."[23]

Giving further reinforcement to one of my major themes in this book—that religious people, not secularists, developed the principle of the separation of church and state—we need to note that Madison studied for the ministry. His work under John Witherspoon at the College of New Jersey (Princeton) started him on the intellectual road that led him to construct a government that provided for both political and religious freedom with as little interference from government as possible in both spheres.

From his academic studies, honed by unceasing reading and worked out actively in the political arena, Madison structured some major themes for his life in terms of church and state:

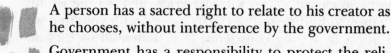

A person has a sacred right to relate to his creator as he chooses, without interference by the government.

Government has a responsibility to protect the religious freedom of its citizens but must not interfere with what a person believes.

No one denomination or religious community could be allowed to dominate the others.[24]

As early as 1774, Madison wrote his life-long friend William Bradford, "Pray for liberty of conscience to all." Throughout his long career, Madison maintained his views on the benefit of religious freedom and the separation of church and state—for both institutions. Late in his life he wrote to his friend Robert Walsh with whom Madison conducted a steady correspondence:

> It was the Universal opinion of the Century preceding the last, that Civil Government could not stand without the prop of a Religious establishment, and that the Christian religion itself, would perish if not supported by a legal provision for its Clergy. The experience of Virginia conspicuously corroborates the disproof of both opinions. The Civil Government, tho' bereft of everything like an associated hierarchy, possesses the requisite stability and performs its functions with complete success; whilst the number, the industry, and the morality of the Priesthood, and the devotion of the people have been manifestly increased by the total separation of the Church from the State.[25]

At age eighty-one, both looking back at the American experience and looking forward with vision sharpened by practical experience, Madison summed up his views of church and state relations in a letter to a "Reverend Adams"

> I must admit moreover that it may not be easy, in every possible case, to trace the line of separation between the rights of religion and the Civil authority with such distinctness as to avoid collisions and doubts on unessential points. The tendency of a usurpation on one side or the other, or to a corrupting coalition or alliance between them, will be best guarded by an entire abstinence of the Government from interference in any way whatever, beyond the necessity of preserving public order, and protecting each sect against trespass on its legal rights by others.[26]

I will resist the temptation to give highlights of the views of some of the other Founding Fathers such as John Jay and Alexander Hamilton. Suffice it to say they generally agreed with their enlightened peers.

From this brief overview, it is clear that Thomas Jefferson and James Madison provided the carefully thought-out philosophical framework for religious liberty and the separation of church and state. Their ideas did not make it perfectly into the Constitution and Bill of Rights, but, more than any other school of thought on the relationship between church and state, their views prevailed and shaped the young nation's self-understanding of religious liberty. The historical fact that Jeffersonian/Madisonian ideas carried the day provides encouragement, if not documentable proof, that the opinion makers in the constitutional era held firmly to complete religious liberty underpinned by some configuration of the separation of church and state.

If the separation of church and state was a novel idea among Americans, it was a radical idea among the family of nations who watched the birth pangs of the United States. European rulers could not imagine governing in a state that did not have an official religion. Kings and prime ministers looked to religion to keep order, provide some pageantry in the otherwise dull lives of most people, and give moral and divine legitimacy to the regime. By any measure, European rulers regarded religion as a tool of the state, there to support the regime. How could the new government manage without the backing of the church? It would never work, they forecast. All too often, largely because of the "kept" nature of much state religion, religious faith has lacked vitality and made only minimal differences in the moral or spiritual lives of the people. Now, thanks to the vision of the men and women who thought about and labored for the creation of our country, and the passions for complete freedom in politics and pulpit that animated the people, this country's religious freedom stands out as the standard for men and women everywhere who yearn to express their deepest impulses without interference from the state or official church.

CHAPTER FIVE

European Roots
of Religious Liberty

R eligious people have a notorious record for intolerance, despite the fact that most religious writings teach under-standing and appreciation of the points of views of others, and despite the fact that most religions, at one time or another, have themselves suffered persecution and intolerance. We have a difficult time learning history's lessons.

For instance, at the heart of Christianity is Jesus' invitation, "Whosoever *will* may come." He never compelled anyone to choose his way. The holy books of Judaism, Hinduism, Islam, and the other world religions contain similar notes of volun-tariness and openness. The story of religion, however, is strewn with accounts of forced conversions from one religion to an-other, depending on the faith of the conqueror at a given time. The problem, then, of intolerance lies not with the particular religions, their founders and teaching, but with the people who take up this or that path to religious truth. The believers, not the beliefs, pose the threat to freedom.

The early Christian church, absorbed as it was with survival, did not give much attention to religious liberty. Indeed, the Christians came to know the deadly sting of intolerance from the Jews and Romans among whom they lived. These early Christians evangelized all over the Roman world, but in the early annals of the Church, one finds no records of forced conversions. Those would come later. To the contrary, Paul, Peter, and the other leaders of the church time and again made the point that only heartfelt commitment to Jesus made any real difference.

During its first three centuries, Christianity flourished as a faith that attracted people looking for a better life here on earth as well as a promise of full existence beyond the grave. Generous acts of nobility and kindness mark those opening centuries of the Christian movement. Problems of intolerance toward others ripped at the Church when separation between church and state broke down.

Through a fascinating process (beyond the scope of this book), Christianity became the officially established religion of the Roman Empire under Constantine, beginning in about 313 A.D. In a short period of time, Christians, who had been on the outside of culture and influence looking in, moved, if you please, to the inside. Christian leaders gained access to places of power. They became policy makers, people of authority, sought after by the high and mighty. In this process the Roman Catholic Church gradually assumed a status of preeminence among the churches of the fading Empire. By the end of the fourth century A.D. Christianity reached two significant plateaus: The various church councils essentially finalized the canon of the scriptures and establishment Christianity began to focus on dissidents in a way that was outside its way of thinking about, and practicing, religion. And religion's ancient story repeated itself: The persecuted became the persecutors.

Historian Henry Kamen writes in The Rise of Toleration:

> By the end of the fourth century the Church had grown to accept the exercise of punitive constraint against heterodox Christians, and Catholics looked with approval on the measures taken by the secular authorities against Arians and Donatists. As the established religion, Christianity was drawn irresistibly towards an alliance of interest with the secular power. Despite the regular protests of distinguished prelates, the new Church/State alliance began a programme of selective persecution.[1]

In the course of time, the Church turned almost exclusively to the state as the agent for enforcing religious orthodoxy. Even great men of faith and learning like Augustine of Hippo appealed to the secular powers for aid in suppressing groups they regarded as heretics.

With the final sigh and collapse of the Roman Empire in the fifth and sixth centuries, and the descending of the chaotic Dark Ages on Europe for several hundred years, the Roman Catholic Church moved into the power vacuum, becoming both a spiritual and temporal force. Especially during the reign of powerful popes like Leo III, who crowned Charlemagne in 800 A.D., Gregory VII in the late eleventh century, and Innocent III in the early thirteenth century, life in Western Europe took on the caste of a church state. Popes raised armies, forced local rulers and their subjects to make obeisance, excommunicated kings and kingdoms in retaliation for rebellion, and in every way forsook their humble Master's teaching about peace and non-violence. Popes could have such free reign during these centuries of the Middle Ages because European states existed only as shadows of what they would become in the fifteenth and sixteenth centuries and thereafter. The Universal Church had no serious organized competition for political power during this era as national states struggled to get themselves together. True, the Holy Roman Empire existed on paper as a way to unify Christendom politically, but only rarely did the titular emperor have any significant power.

During these centuries, and indeed until the American era, heresy in religion was regarded as treason to the state. Thomas Aquinas thought that recalcitrants from the Church deserved the death penalty if they persisted in their views. Banishment, hanging, burning became the fates of men and women who dared question the all-powerful ways of the ecclesiastical powers. Frequently popes or bishops possessed, themselves, the police forces to carry out punishments against dissenters, but these clerics did not hesitate to demand that the secular forces hurl the death-dealing thunderbolts when such methods seemed expedient.

Nothing lasts forever, except change. Beginning in the fourteenth century, the practical dictatorship of the Church began to face serious challenges. As a sense of national identity infused the peoples of the various states, the power of their kings increased. For instance, France and the kings of France grew stronger, diminishing the influence of the Holy Roman Emperor and the Pope. French philosophers questioned the necessity for one European empire. Individual kingdoms carved out their own dominions. The Pope could rule over the church, saving souls, but kings would tend to the political and temporal needs of their own peoples.

As Europe began to awake from its centuries-long slumber, myriad religious and cultural forces gradually converged to create the Renaissance of the fifteenth and sixteenth centuries. The singular view of the world as imposed by the church came under attack. A lay-led, anti-clerical spirit began to emerge which questioned the assumption that all wisdom resided in the clergy. This new, inquiring spirit searched for universal human values—quests that took men and women outside their long-accepted religiously dominated culture. Within Catholicism the views of Erasmus and Thomas More, called the Christian humanists, challenged the entrenched views and methods of the papacy and religious orders.

Martin Luther, the young German monk, gathered up the growing force of the Renaissance and, without intending to, unleashed the Protestant Reformation in 1519 when he nailed his Ninety-five Theses on the church door at Wittenberg. Luther's movement, which found important echoes in other parts of Europe, broke the religious monopoly that had prevailed for a thousand years.

Ironically, while Luther emphasized the freedom of the Christian person before God, he had almost no concept of practical religious liberty. He looked to the princes to enforce religious orthodoxy on the people. The German monarchs who left the Catholic Church, and to whom Luther turned frequently, moved with ruthlessness and intolerance toward dissenters, especially to those who chose to remain loyal to the Pope. Once Protestantism became the official religion of the various kingdoms, the secular and religious leaders expected everyone to fall in line. Those who refused to comply faced persecution, banishment, or death.

Almost paralleling Luther's movement in Germany, John Calvin, a Frenchman who migrated to Geneva, began to write and teach. Calvin emphasized individual responsibility for one's relationship to God. He relied heavily on Augustine's concept of the Kingdom of God, extrapolating from the Kingdom idea his notion of the godly society. If Luther's movement emphasized the state church, Calvin recreated the medieval idea of the church state. Government existed to promote the faith. Rulers had the responsibility to encourage faithfulness as well as to maintain places of worship. Calvin, quite apart from his great learning and power of persuasion, had no compunction against using the power of the state to enforce orthodoxy. His willingness to use secular power to demand religious orthodoxy reached a horrible focus in the execution of Servetus, the Unitarian dissenter.

Perhaps we ask too much of Luther and Calvin when we deplore their lack of generosity toward dissenters. As far-thinking as they were, they nonetheless lived in their own time. Freedom of any kind was a rare commodity in their day. But if they did not encourage religious liberty overtly, Lutheranism and Calvinism laid some of the foundations on which later generations of thinkers would build as peoples and their governments stumbled toward a freedom to practice faith without government interference.

By any measure, the Reformation became one of the major tributaries that flowed into the American experiment in complete religious freedom. Specifically, the Reformation's emphasis on the sovereignty of God, the right of the person to rely on the Bible alone, and the gradual decentralization of the church establishments contained the seeds of religious freedom.

Concurrently with Luther and Calvin, who used temporal powers to implement their ideas, a group of political and religious dissidents who were considered highly radical in their time began to emerge. The best known of those who chose to carve out their own way were the Anabaptists. Their name came about as a slur: They renounced their own infant baptism, insisting rather that valid baptism came only after a conversion experience. They insisted on being baptized *again* (*ana*—from the Greek).

The Anabaptists of Central Europe caused the most public revulsion and received the worst persecution for their religious radicalism. The roots of this approach to faith reached back to one of the important strains of the early church; it emphasized personal conversion to Jesus and the baptism of believers, thus rejecting the ancient and uncritically accepted practice of infant baptism. For the Anabaptists the church came into being as believers created communities of faith in Jesus. They rejected the pervasive notion of a church defined by the borders of the municipality or of the state. Their view of the church necessitated a separation between church and state. Many of the Anabaptists rejected violence and wars as evil tools of the state.

Established religion and government persecuted the Anabaptists ruthlessly, although almost no evidence exists to suggest they posed any threat to the social order. These "strange" believers simply wanted to be left alone to live their religion as they understood it.

As the sixteenth century progressed, the realities of practical politics made changes on many fronts inevitable. Catholics, Lutherans, and Calvinists living side by side in the various countries gradually pushed European society toward toleration, though change proved tediously slow. The spirit of nationalism grew stronger, creating nations out of hitherto small duchies and city-states and forcing their rulers to yearn and work for religious as well as political harmony.

Since the American story is closely linked to France and England, we do well to pay close attention to the evolution of toleration in both those countries.

France managed to avoid many of the effects of the Protestant Reformation. A series of strong Catholic kings preserved the faith in France. But France had its reformationists, called the Huguenots. For thirty years France was torn by religious warfare; then King Henry IV, a Protestant, converted to Catholicism in 1593, saying, "Paris is worth a Mass." As a way to secure the political and economic stability of his country, Henry set about to grant limited religious freedom to Protestants without taking away any more than necessary from the Catholic clergy. In 1597, King Henry issued the Edict of Nantes, which granted carefully circumscribed religious freedom to the Protestants. Under the edict the Huguenots could worship in certain areas of the country, though they had to pay taxes to support the Catholic Church and had to observe all the Catholic feasts and celebrations. Protestants gained a limited right to manage the affairs of their churches. They likewise gained admission to universities, schools, and hospitals and theoretically could hold office.

As is often the case in such compromises, the edict satisfied no one and angered everyone. The Huguenots complained because the ruling gave them so little, while Catholics complained because it gave so much. But the Edict of Nantes stands as a milestone on the road to the ideal of a free church in a free state. Henry demonstrated great courage and liberality, which places him among the great rulers of history.

Unfortunately, King Louis XIV, under pressure from the Roman Catholic hierarchy, revoked the Edict of Nantes in 1685, causing 200,000 Huguenots to flee to Protestant lands. Many came to the American colonies where they became influential in government and commerce.

A Century and a half earlier, King Henry VIII of England had brought about the reformation of the English church not from religious motives but out of political considerations. True, he wanted to marry Anne Bolyen and Pope Clement VII would not give him a divorce from Catherine of Aragon, so he simply moved English religion out from under the control of the Holy Father and made himself the Protector of the Faith. But other reasons also prompted him to the move. As one of the strongest kings in English history, riding the crest of the spirit of change and reformation in Europe, he took this opportunity to seize control of the power and wealth of the church in his own land.

For several decades, after Henry's pull away from Rome, England passed through several phases of its reformation, during which there were periods of persecution for both Protestants and Catholics. Finally, by 1689, the new Protestant monarchs, William and Mary, issued, more for political then religious reasons, the Act of Toleration; it granted a measure of freedom to the several types of Protestants in the land. Even Baptists and Quakers won the protection of the new law, except in regard to holding public office, a privilege reserved for members of the established Church of England. And even in 1689

Catholics, Unitarians, and Jews did not come under the benefits
of the act but remained subject to punishment for their religious
beliefs.

History does not provide many neat points of demarcation.
Great movements and events run concurrently with, collide,
and fold into each other. The American approach to life emerged
as a product of powerful political and religious forces that rumbled through England and Europe as English and Continental
settlers made their way to these shores. Our forebears shaped
these powerful forces to the benefit of the American experience
in religious liberty.

CHAPTER SIX

American Colonial Experience with Church and State

We Americans take great pride in remembering that many of our ancestors came to these shores fleeing religious persecution and seeking to establish freedom of worship for themselves. The search for religious freedom provided a major impulse for much of the settlement that took place in the earliest years of the seventeenth century, particularly in New England. Our imagination takes flight as we travel back through the time tunnel to feel the powerful emotions that must have surged through the Pilgrims as they bobbed in their tiny boat off the shores of Massachusetts, solemnly signing the Mayflower Compact.

Having come from England, these Christians honored the British king, but they wanted to separate themselves entirely from the English church. When life in England proved untenable to this tiny band, they moved to America. Offshore from Plymouth, on November 11, 1620, the forty-one male passengers entered into the Mayflower Compact, a document that stands out as the *first* written constitution in history. This voluntary agreement passed on to civil life the democratic principles by which the Pilgrims operated their church life.

In the spirit of the Compact the Pilgrims of Plymouth created a rather generous and liberal society. Under William Bradford, who served as governor for twenty-five years, the colony avoided much of the intolerance and rigidity that characterized their Puritan cousins in the nearby Massachusetts Bay Colony. Unfortunately for the spirit of tolerance and openness, in due time the Massachusetts Bay Colony absorbed the Plymouth Colony and its larger-minded Pilgrims.

Despite the appeal of the Pilgrims, the main story of the struggle for religious freedom in New England revolves around the Puritans. Whatever else one may say in a negative way about the Puritans, their courage and grit can never be doubted. These brave Christian souls endured terrible suffering to establish their homes and churches. Their religious fervor almost alone kept them alive as they struggled with all the problems of life in a new, lush but harsh country. And they reveled in religious freedom. No king or ecclesiastical council told them how to conduct their religious lives. Relying on their own understanding of scripture, these hardy settlers created their own forms for church life.

One major problem did occur: The Puritans refused to grant religious freedom to fellow settlers who dissented from the community's religious norms. It frequently comes as a shock to twentieth-century Americans to realize that full religious freedom for all people was an unheard-of luxury in early colonial America, especially in New England and Virginia. Why?

The settlers who came to New England, especially the Puritans of Massachusetts, built their society on the philosophy and theology of John Calvin, the reformationist who turned the city of Geneva into a church state. Calvin taught that the state existed to enforce true religion. The state had the divinely ordained responsibility to maintain churches where the word of God was correctly preached.

Following the teachings of Calvin, the Massachusetts settlers created a church state ruled on theocratic principles. For all practical purposes church and state were synonymous. In 1631, the legislative body of the colony, the General Court, ruled that only members of the church, the Congregational Church, could serve in that assembly. With this rule, the clergy, who alone could decide on church membership, gained effective control of the state. As somewhat of a check and balance, a clergyman could not serve as a magistrate, nor could a magistrate serve as a clergyman.

Reflecting the teachings of Calvin, the church members expected the magistrate, the government, to enforce public worship and deal with heresy. Government should curb sin because of its threat to life and property.

In this church state, the leaders had no thought of human equality and brooked no dissent. The Puritans had such a strong notion that they alone possessed the true revelation of the word of God that they could not conceive of allowing others to exist freely in their midst who obviously denied the truth. Toleration of unbelief offended God and harmed society.

The General Court levied a tax for the support of the churches and clergy. Failure or refusal to pay landed one in jail. Thus, the majority, having suffered intolerably in England for the right to practice their own faith, could not see beyond their own parochialism to grant that same freedom to minorities within their midst.

But even in that tightly run society, the separation between church and state began to peek through. Over a period of several years, distinctive functions between the two institutions came to be established. The General Court, with an eye to community order, asked the ministers to draw up statements of faith that would be presented to the Court for approval. The legislature did not undertake to draw up the statement, leaving that task to the ministers, but did relegate to itself the right to give final approval.

Only as the original settlers died off did Massachusetts move toward increased democracy and more separation between church and state—and then, ever so slowly. In fact, Massachusetts became the last state in the Union to give up an established church. Not until 1833, some forty years after the ratification of the First Amendment, did the state disestablish the Congregational Church as its official church.

We should note that, in time, reality overtook the ideal in Massachusetts as in other colonies. Though Congregationalism remained the established church, other Christian groups began to grow, demanding their place in the sun. Especially Baptists, some Quakers, and Unitarians simply intruded their way into the life of the colony. The Congregationalist establishment complained and kept up a running battle with the dissenters, but the tides of time and change demanded an ever-increasing tolerance to people of different religious persuasion. Lest we be too hard on our ancestors, we have to remember that most people of the early seventeenth century could not conceive of religious liberty. The American experiment was still so young. Only the most enlightened visionaries reached beyond their times to talk about toleration and liberty.

If a Calvinistic Congregationalism dominated the religious life of early colonial New England, the Church of England exerted the most force in the southern colonies, especially Virginia. By the beginning of the 1640s, the Bishop of London decided he would also be Bishop of Virginia. Actually, the London bishop never had much power in Virginia because of the distance between the two portions of his diocese. In addition, the Virginians, though loyal to the British crown, early on decided that they more than possessed the requisite talents to run their own religious affairs. The Church of England in Virginia in reality became the State Church of Virginia, no less established and officially part of the state, but quite independent from the English church. At one point, the Bishop of London tried to dispatch a bishop to Virginia, but his efforts met with such resistance that he withdrew his efforts.

As in New England, all taxpayers of Virginia paid to support the religious establishment, and this included dissenters who did not want to associate with the state church. Also, from time to time, colonial authorities exercised their power to make all clergy register in order to conduct their ministerial duties.[1] The sight of Baptist ministers in jail for refusing to register with the government pricked the consciences of such men as Thomas Jefferson and James Madison, pushing them further in their thinking about religious liberty and the separation of the church from the state.

In the Carolinas and Georgia, the English church had official status but there the British authorities had even less influence than they did in Virginia. Again, distance, a scattered population, the lack of officially ordained clergy, and the growing American sense of independence made any kind of direct control all but impossible. Dissenters, the Baptists, Presbyterians, etc., had much more religious freedom there despite the official status of the Church of England.

But the colonial religious scene was not all so bleak. Rhode Island in New England and the Middle Colonies told a much better, though not perfect, story.

Rhode Island shone as the one bright spot in New England, thanks to the incredibly far-sighted thinking of Roger Williams. We have talked about him before, and will again, but we need to focus on him at this point.

Indissolubly linked to the saga of religious liberty and the separation of church and state is the name of Roger Williams. Our understanding of this unique man's contribution to political and religious liberty has grown through the years. In his own time, as a radical dissenter from the church state of Massachusetts he was so far ahead of his time as to be almost ineffective.

Williams had hardly landed in Boston after sailing from England, before he began to take exception with the repressive religious and political climate he encountered. He immediately started agitating for more democracy in church government. And he uttered the heresy that no official linkage should exist between church and state. In 1635, the General Court convicted Williams of "disseminating new and dangerous opinions," banishing him from the colony.[2] Williams, along with some other dissenters, founded the colony of Rhode Island and trumpeted, perhaps for the first time in history, that all human beings who chose to live in this community would enjoy full political and religious freedom—even the Indians. In 1639 he founded a Baptist church in Providence, although he did not long remain a Baptist.[3]

Williams most clearly enunciated what became the American principle of the separation of church and state, a doctrine he espoused to save the church from the world's corruption. In this context he introduced his "wall" idea, which, as we have seen, may have been the genesis of Jefferson".[4]

Williams's passion for liberty came out of the fervor and depths of his own religious devotion: What man can fully know the mind and message of God? What right does one human being have to compel another to belief? What is conversion worth at gunpoint? What good is obedience to the truth when the stocks are waiting if you disagree? Williams insisted on religious freedom because he could not bear the thought that the love of God should be forced on anyone.

The Middle Colonies—New York, New Jersey, Pennsylvania, Delaware—had anything but a homogeneous religious establishment. Into these colonies poured people with a wide variety of religious convictions. Quakers, Moravians, Reformed, Baptists, Mennonites, Lutherans, Roman Catholics, and a few Jews settled these areas, ensuring, by their diversity, greater toleration.

Under the influence of the religiously tolerant Dutch, New Amsterdam (later New York) early granted a large measure of religious freedom. The irascible Peter Stuyvesant tried to establish the Dutch Reformed Church, but his efforts failed. Christians of all faiths could practice with little interference by the authorities.

Lord Cecilius Calvert, son of Maryland's founder, Lord George Calvert, completed his father's dream of a place where persecuted Catholics could live in peace. Williams came to religious toleration from a carefully thought-out theology; the Calverts came to toleration from much more practical considerations. As Roman Catholic colonists under a Protestant king, the only way the Calverts could make a haven for their fellow Catholics was to welcome Protestants as well. The net effect was a colony where people of all faiths could practice their religious faith with little interference from the government. To make his point even more emphatically, Cecilius issued the Act of Toleration of 1649, giving toleration to all Christians sects except Unitarians. Ironically, Unitarians and Jews did not gain full political and religious freedom in Maryland until 1826.

Before we get too carried away about freedom in Maryland, we should note that one's Christianity had to be trinitarian and that the state could impose civil and criminal punishments for religious impiety. But, especially when compared to New England and Virginia, Maryland shines as a place of freedom and tranquility.

The third great hero of religious liberty for this early colonial period is William Penn, the rich and powerful English Quaker who founded the colony of Pennsylvania. Of all the dissenting groups in seventeenth-century England, none received harsher treatment than the Quakers. George Fox, the founder of the Quaker movement, believed that God revealed himself to all people and that therefore all people were directly responsible to God and had no need of church or clergy. Naturally this belief put him at odds with the state church of England.

An immediate outgrowth of this belief in universal revelation was religious toleration. If God had made himself known to everyone, then no one should be discriminated against. Furthermore, because all people shared the light of God, the Quakers evolved as strong believers in democracy.

The first beachhead for Quakerism in America was New Jersey, though they shortly lost out to forces partial to the Church of England. But the Quaker experiment in government and religion in New Jersey emboldened the powerful William Penn to persuade the Duke of York to give him Pennsylvania in exchange for a debt of £16,000 owed to his father by the government.[5] Without hesitation, Penn decreed full religious toleration for all sects, transforming the colony of Pennsylvania into a haven for the oppressed from Europe as well as from other American colonies. Unfortunately, even in enlightened Pennsylvania, Catholics had a difficult time. They could neither vote nor hold office. However, they could build churches and worship as they chose, and thus Catholic life in Pennsylvania was much better than in most other colonies.

A strong case can be made that Pennsylvania rapidly became America's strongest colony because of this spirit of religious and intellectual freedom. Benjamin Franklin's spirit of inquiry and enterprise found a welcome counterpart in Philadelphia, along with many other of the New World's brightest minds. Indeed, "The doors of Pennsylvania were open to the world of men and of ideas, and the eighteenth century entered America through the port of Philadelphia."[6]

The story of religious liberty during the early colonial period cannot be completed without talking about dissenting religious groups. Up and down the seaboard, Baptists, Presbyterians,

Catholics, Quakers, and other Christian groups chafed under official establishment churches. These groups—especially the Baptists—began to push for religious freedom for themselves. In the earliest days, the dissenters craved only to be left alone. They did not question the reality of state churches. They paid their taxes for the support of the established church as a part of life. But as the spirit of freedom grew brighter in the land, as talk of independence from England became more widespread, emboldened by the likes of Roger Williams and William Penn the dissenters began to beat their drums for, first, official toleration and then for the separating of the power of the state from control of the churches. It took the dissenters decades to achieve their mission. But perseverance paid off. As the seventeenth century gave way to the eighteenth, intellectual giants like George Mason, Thomas Jefferson, and James Madison came on the scene and began to give form to the aspirations for freedom that had stirred an ever-growing number of colonial Americans.

ie 1600's

1700's

Among those early dissenters, the Baptists stand out as the strongest contenders for religious freedom and separation of churches from the control of the state. In early colonial America, Baptists were a distinct religious minority. From the earliest days of their meager beginnings in England, the Baptists preached toleration and the separation of church and state. They brought those twin principles with them to America. As a distinctively minority faith in New England and Virginia, the Baptists at first dreamed only of toleration. Nevertheless, as time went by, Baptist leaders, following the example of Roger Williams, began to emphasize the separation of church and state.

The net effect of this lesson in history is to show that the push for religious freedom and the separation between church and state is not the invention of modern jurisprudence. Thousands in colonial America, with a passion for freedom in every area of their lives, dreamed of religious freedom. Particularly those who gave allegiance to the non-established churches gradually came to realize that their dream of liberty could come about only as the church and state operated in different spheres.

The broad sweep of colonial religious history shows that religious freedom and the separation of church and state did not come from a secularist mindset or from a declining, drooping religious commitment. Church/state separation arose because this political vehicle provided the greatest amount of religious freedom to the largest number of people. Religious freedom and church/state separation paved the road to religious peace in America. The new nation could come into being without religious strife. Religious toleration and the separation of church and state, particularly in the Middle Colonies of New York and Pennsylvania, facilitated the birth of a nation at peace with itself religiously.

In the magnificent decades of the eighteenth century that led up to the American Revolution and the creation of a new country, men like Jefferson and Madison would declare that the state, the magistrates, and the political rulers lacked the "competence" to judge over matters of the heart and spirit. The seventeenth-century American colonials who worshipped outside the establishment religions lacked the vision or the language to describe what would be, but they longed for that kind of atmosphere of freedom. In due time, the religious and political climate would emerge that would bring Jefferson and his ilk to the fore to make religious liberty and church/state separation a political reality.

Freedom of Religious PRACTICE,
PRACTICE = Belief AND Practice/behavior
Belief = internal but also expressed
Practice = behavior, ritual
The market Place — can cary internal belief, expressions
with limits ie r proselitize at work
without permission
— Behavior—Ritual cannot force on
others

CHAPTER SEVEN

The Constitutional Debate

O f a class of seminary students, I inquired, "How many times does the U.S. Constitution mention the name of God?" After a moment of puzzled silence, some of the students began making stabbing guesses. Finally, one young man said, rather hesitantly, "I don't think 'God' is mentioned in the Constitution."

How would you have answered? You would have been on target if you had agreed with the last student.

The men who gathered in Philadelphia in the summer of 1787 to redraft the Articles of Confederation, or come up with a new governing document, mirrored the culture and religion of the new nation. Some held deep religious convictions while others gave little evidence of a religious point of view. An appreciation for religion, mixed with anxieties about the divisive power of religion, marked the representatives to the convention.

As the convention struggled with its work, Benjamin Franklin, as we have already noted, suggested that the delegates begin their daily sessions with prayer. Others in the delegation questioned that practice. Lacking funds to pay chaplains, wishing to avoid religious divisiveness, worrying lest word of prayer meetings send a signal of uncertainty and deadlock out of the deliberations, the convention decided to do its work without benefit of spoken prayers.

Any serious reading of the events of the summer of 1787 reveals that most of the framers took a decidedly secular view of their work, although they welcomed prayers and frequented the churches of the city. The delegates realized they were constructing a document for men by men. This all-together-remarkable collection of lawyers, businessmen, clergy, tradesmen, and farmers had no notion of creating a theocracy. Being people of their time—a time when religion held an important but *proper* place—they gave religion every due consideration, worked from a world view that held religion in high esteem, but strove to create a document that would govern not simply the religious lives but the total lives of the people. My point in this lesson in constitutional history is to say that the Founding Fathers did not intend to create a "Christian nation"; that is, a nation that would try simply to play back certain teachings of the Bible.

Among the several key players in Philadelphia, James Madison of Virginia took the lead. It was he who had so recently outmaneuvered Patrick Henry and his assessments for religion bill, who had managed to persuade the Virginia General Assembly to pass Jefferson's Statute on Religion Freedom. Though the delegates did not spend a great deal of time discussing religious freedom that summer, we can assume that Madison kept a keen eye on issues of religion as they played into the formation of the Constitution.

Another Virginian, George Mason, the author of Virginia's original Bill of Rights, which included the first statement on religious freedom in the country, likewise watched the development of the document for its impact on religious freedom.

Those fifty-five men could not have imagined the religious diversity that would begin to characterize the new country in less than a hundred years, but they did determine that the government *as the government* would not single out any religion as special. In fact, they drafted a document that provided for a government that was neutral when it came to religion. The country and the people could be as religious as it/they chose, but the government as government would maintain a stance of appreciative neutrality toward religion and religions.

Political reasons kept religious debate to a minimum. Since most of the states had some form of official religion, the delegates did not want to sink the new Constitution on the rocks of religious divisiveness. Apparently they adopted the adage "The least said is the easiest mended."

Even though the First Amendment had not yet been born, the delegates, reflecting the growing consensus among Americans, held to the cardinal principle that church and state must be kept separate.[1] They ascribed to the not-very-old, American-born notion that religion should fund itself. The delegates, in that pre-federal era, rather uncritically accepted the assumption that religion was a matter for local option.[2]

The only reference to religion in the Constitution itself is Article VI: "No religious test shall ever be required as a qualification to any office or public trust under the United States." This article deals with religion in a negative way, placing limitations on the role and power of religion in the official life of the nation. With amazingly little debate, the Constitutional Convention bequeathed a "principle to the American political system that revolutionized its future."[3] This article provided for the separation of church and state. In fact, Madison argued that the inclusion of the article in the Constitution, linked with his concept that religious freedom was already implicitly protected in the document, made a direct statement on religious liberty unnecessary.

Charles Pinckney, today an all-but-forgotten delegate from South Carolina, introduced the article to the Convention. This bright but rather pompous South Carolinian, though a member of the aristocracy of his state, took a surprising interest in religious liberty. Despite his membership in the established Anglican Church, he stood up for Quakers, Roman Catholics, and dissenting Protestants. When time came to ratify the Constitution, and later the Bill of Rights, Pinckney fought a good and successful fight in his native state.

With the inclusion of this article in the new Constitution, the delegates took a leap for freedom that catapulted them beyond most of their states. At the time of the Revolution, all the thirteen states had religious tests for office that reserved public office for Protestants. Though the national sentiment was softening, when the Constitutional Convention met, Jews, Catholics, Unitarians, agnostics, freethinkers and atheists could not hold public office in any state, and, in most, could not serve on juries.[4]

From our vantage point of two centuries of history, given the existence of the states' already-existing religious tests, it seems startling indeed that Article VI would have been proposed, much less pass so easily. Luther Martin of Maryland reported that the convention adopted the article without much debate.[5] Some anti-constitutionalists used the article and the absence of any mention of God as ammunition to seek defeat of the entire document, but tolerance and good sense led the nation to accept the Constitution, complete with Article VI.

To their credit, beginning with Delaware in 1792, most of the states adopted the language of Article VI and banned religious tests. Two states, however, held out. The North Carolina legislature clung to its belief in God and the Protestant-religion test until 1868. Tiny New Hampshire hung on to its religious tests until 1946! Time and again, courageous leaders came forth to advocate the revocation of the religious test, only to meet failure. Finally in 1946, New Hampshire's state constitution was brought into line with the federal document. "To be sure, the act had become a dead letter. But its retention was a symbol of bigotry."[6]

But, if the framers of the Constitution kept a healthy official distance between religion and the government they envisioned, they nonetheless kept alive their own religious commitments. A history of the summer shows that many of the framers attended religious services. A study of their letters reveals many references to God, to the need for divine guidance, to a plea for the people back home to pray for their deliberations. This is the proper balance, the separation between church and state in microcosm. The government, as government, should and ought to be neutral, appreciative perhaps, but non-supportive, especially with money and official influence toward religion.

People in government can work out of the framework of their own religious convictions as they see fit, knowing full well that the voters will render ultimate judgment on the way those religious convictions get translated into public policy.

The fateful summer of 1787 drew to a close. After intense debate, countless hours of behind-the-scene maneuvering, the framers had their document. Monday, September 17, 1787, dawned cool and clear in Philadelphia. Delegates gathered in Independence Hall for what they sensed would be the day of signing.

After the Constitution was read in its entirety to the assembly, Benjamin Franklin addressed his colleagues:

> Mr. President, I confess that there are several parts of this constitution which I do not at present approve. But I am not sure I shall never approve them. For having lived long, I have experienced many instances of being obliged by better information or fuller consideration, to change opinions even on important subjects, which I once thought right, but found to be otherwise.[7]

The grand old doctor continued: "In these sentiments, Sir, I agree to this Constitution with all its faults, if they are such."

As a hush fell over the room, thirty-eight men from twelve states signed the United States Constitution. For reasons of history that appeared good to the leaders of the State of Rhode Island, they had chosen to stay away from the convention.

After one of the most remarkable and productive summers in the history of the human race, the U.S. Constitution, complete with all its majesty and compromise, received the necessary votes to hand it back to the Continental Congress meeting in New York. That congress then voted to send the document out to the states for ratification or rejection.

Up and down the Atlantic Seaboard the states addressed the problem of the new document, and the ratification process provides one of history's great lessons on self-government. Heated debate rarely gave way to rowdiness or bloodshed. By the summer of 1788, the Constitution had become the law of the land

and its various provisions for government were being set in motion.

Out of the debate, however, one vital element had emerged: The country demanded a Bill of Rights. Especially in Virginia, a Bill of Rights, including a provision for the protection of religious liberty, became a crucial trade-off necessary for ratification. George Mason of Virginia, one of religious liberty's earliest and staunchest proponents, refused to support the new Constitution for several reasons, not the least of which was because it lacked a Bill of Rights, including a statement on religious freedom.

Among the first items of business for the First Congress, when it convened in the city of Philadelphia in January 1789, was the introduction of a Bill of Rights.

Even though he did not think a Bill of Rights necessary, Madison had made pledges during the ratification process that he would introduce a slate of liberty-strengthening amendments. Accordingly, on May 4, 1789, just four days after Washington's first inauguration as President, Madison announced to the House of Representatives that he would introduce a Bill of Rights.

As debate on religious liberty language progressed, the Senate proposed: "Congress shall make no law establishing any particular denomination of religion in preference to another." The House of Representatives settled on a religious-liberty statement that said: "Congress shall make no law establishing religion, or to prevent the free exercise thereof, or to infringe the rights of conscience." The Senate refined the proposed amendment to read: "CONGRESS SHALL MAKE NO LAW RESPECTING AN ESTABLISHMENT OF RELIGION OR PROHIBITING THE FREE EXERCISE THEREOF." This was the wording that prevailed.

The First Congress wanted a government neutral toward the idea of religion, not just neutral toward religions. We stand in amazement at how much freedom and balance the First Congress packed into only sixteen words.

A study of that summer-long debate, particularly if that debate is set in the context of the time, teaches that the statement on religious liberty did not represent the victory of one school of thought over another. Rather, the clause emerged as a consensus, a compromise, a reflection of feelings more than realities, in the new nation.[8]

The First Congress had a keen understanding of the limitations of its powers. The states would have hands-on control over matters of church and state. The Religion Clauses, when they were written, applied only to the national government. Lest this assertion give diehard states' righters cause for rejoicing, we need to understand that many members of the Congress still felt themselves to be more citizens of their states than of the nation—an attitude that would later cost the nation a bloody civil war.

Several important assumptions underlie the passage of the Religion Clauses:

The United States would have no national religion as its official religion. True, the country thought of itself as Protestant Christian. As we have said, non-Protestants lived with second-class citizenship. Nonetheless, there would be no official religion.

Congress could never make a law aimed at creating or establishing a national religion. "Establishment" carried with it the idea that government would prefer one religion over another. Though many of the states did, at first, express preferences, the amendment would prevent the federal government from ever engaging in such favoritism. The national government would not, in any way, attempt to fund religious enterprises.

The members of the First Congress had no notion of injuring religion. Rather, Judge Joseph Story says that the intention was to "exclude rivalry among Christian sects and to prevent any national ecclesiastical establishment which should give to any hierarchy the exclusive patronage of the national government."[9]

The House and Senate agreed on all the changes to the religious clauses and to the other amendments in the Bill of Rights and passed them on September 25, 1789. A sufficient number of states ratified the Bill of Rights so that they became part of the U.S. Constitution in 1791.

The Congress set the statements about religious freedom in the First Amendment on purpose. Freedom of religion entails freedom of speech, press, assembly, and the right to complain to the government about grievances, personal and societal. By this placement, Congress declared that, indeed, freedom of religion is the First Freedom from which all others flow.

Madison, and the others who paid such close attention to the First Amendment, did not try to offer precise definitions of religious freedom and the separation of church and state. A. James Reichley of the Brookings Institute says: "Some ambiguity was no doubt present . . . But there is nothing in it inconsistent with the virtually unanimous view among the founders that functional separation between church and state should be maintained without threatening the support and guidance received by republican government from religion."[10]

The amendment, in its stately rhythm and dignity of language, embraced not only its own day but reached into the future. Catholic theologian Thomas J. Curry states: "The two clauses represented a double declaration of what Americans wanted to assert about Church and State."[11] The American people understood the religious clauses to mean they could freely practice their religious faith without government interference, as long as those practices did not unduly disturb public order. The ratifiers of the First Amendment further understood that religion should be supported, personally and financially, only *voluntarily*. Curry explains that the American people "saw government attempts to regulate such support as a usurpation of power, as a violation of liberty of conscience and free exercise of religion, and as falling within the scope of what they termed an establishment of religion."[12]

Americans in general, and Baptists (sticklers for church/state separation) in particular, expressed satisfaction with the amendment. The amendment left in place state church establishments where they existed, though it rather quickly inspired most of the states to provide for religious freedom with no religious preferences or tests for office.

How do we reconcile the obvious drive toward religious freedom and no government interference in religious matters, on the national level, with the states' establishments and religious

tests? Admittedly, not easily. Those who look for excuses to
seek closer ties between church and state can find ammunition
for their cause from some of the debates and actions surrounding the construction and ratification of the Bill of Rights, whereas,
just as surely, those of us who support a strict separation between church and state can, likewise, find what we are looking
for. Fairness and honesty lie in seeking to examine eighteenth-
century events in the context of that century.

The history of the time shows that the lawmakers leaned over
backward to avoid any kind of religious tests or preferences in
the documents that framed the new government. And the citizens of the country readily agreed that the national lawmakers
had struck the right attitude. In everyday life, however, Americans, regarded the United States as a Protestant Christian nation.

Why not? For all its century and half of history, America had
understood itself in religious terms, more specifically in Protestant terms. Several Protestant Christian groups flourished but
Roman Catholics and Jews were in a decided minority and
possessed almost no political or religious power. Some Americans understood that "Mahamotens" existed somewhere in the
world, but these were no factor at all in eighteenth-century life
in the United States. To provide for religious freedom for
"heathens and infidels" made about as much sense as flying to
the moon.

Then, much more than today, a "civil religion" pervaded the
United States. Days of prayer, national thanksgivings, sonorous
religious statements by political leaders, religious instruction in
schools were not so much acts of religious worship as rites of
civil religion, part of the ongoing national drama.

What's more, in its earliest days the nation understood itself
more in terms of the States than in terms of the United. Certainly this debate rumbled underneath the surface of national
life and would all too soon be settled on the field of bloody
combat. The sovereign states could do as they pleased but the
potentially voracious national government would have to be
reined.

Jefferson and Madison, who more than any other national

leaders shaped the public-policy thinking on religious freedom, thought and spoke way ahead of most other Americans. These two men, along with John Leland, a Baptist, and a few of his persuasion, could glimpse the implications of religious freedom for all Americans, but it would take decades for most of their fellow Americans to catch up in their thinking. These few political thinkers were content to get the language in place. Practice would eventually catch up with the ideal. They could wait.

In the midst of today's confusions over church and state, we long for our Founding Fathers to have been more specific. If only they had told us what to do! But if they had tried to be more specific, their efforts to secure our rights would have foundered. Let's be grateful for their efforts and turn ourselves to the task of working out the implications of their vision of religious freedom in today's world.

To conclude this discussion of the religious clauses of the First Amendment, let's talk some more about Thomas Jefferson and his "wall." Some TV preachers, as well as writers, politicians, and, worst of all, Supreme Court Justice William Rehnquist, have sought to pull down the wall by disparaging Jefferson's influence on the First Amendment. A popular bit of historical revisionism that floats around these days goes something like this: Jefferson served as ambassador to France during the writing of the Constitution and the Bill of Rights. He had no hand in their preparation and passage because he was out of the country. Therefore, his metaphor about the "wall of separation" is misplaced and ill-informed because he was living in France and was out of touch.

Tommyrot! Thomas Jefferson was James Madison's mentor. Madison as the chief architect of both the Constitution and the Bill of Rights drew heavily from Jefferson's ideas and kept in regular contact with his fellow Virginian even though the latter lived in France. Volumes of correspondence exist between the two men as they discussed the days' crucial events. Jefferson understood that the First Amendment created a separation between church and state because he, more than most of the

Founders, gave form and substance to the nation's understanding of how the two institutions should best relate in the new nation. Some politicians, lawyers, and preachers subject us to mental cruelty when they disparage Jefferson's interpretation simply because he lived in France during the years of the Constitution's framing.

CHAPTER EIGHT

Moving Along into the Nineteenth Century

Thomas Jefferson issued his "wall" statement on New Year's Day, 1802, enunciating his interpretation of the constitutional relationship between church and state. Church and state would appreciate each other but would function in separate spheres, free, as much as possible, from interference one from the other.

The debates that led up to the U.S. Constitution and the document itself made it plain the government would maintain neutrality toward religion and religions. But ink on paper and solemn votes in ratification conventions did not automatically change the life-style of the individual states.

If America was not officially a Christian nation, its citizens were predominantly Protestant. The Protestant perspective shaped the way the nation felt about itself. At least on the surface, we were a nation that believed in God, that held Jesus Christ in high regard, that felt good citizens should attend church, that practiced the Protestant work ethic. An air of civility and gentility, vaguely rooted in Protestantism, characterized public manners and morals.

If the government maintained neutrality toward religion, the majority of the people were clearly suspicious of Catholics and Jews, while holding in disdain "heathen" religions from Africa and Asia. At every level of national life, one encountered an easy accommodation between church and state. The Christian cross and the American flag were displayed in public places with hardly a voice of dissent raised. The federal courts would not deal with a religious-freedom matter until 1845, and then only by saying they could *not* deal with a religious issue that involved a state rather then the national government.

But the spirit of the new Constitution and its First Amendment began to take hold. Under the strong influence of Virginia and human rights advocates like Mason, Jefferson, and Madison, the southern states quickly moved to rewrite their constitutions and disestablish all churches.

In 1777, Georgia had adopted a constitution that provided for religious freedom, refused to impose a religious test for voters, but limited membership in the legislature to Protestants. This most rural and southern of the original states removed all religious tests in 1789.

South Carolina's 1778 constitution, in considerable detail, established the Protestant religion as the official faith for the state. Only Protestants could sit in the legislature. By 1790, a revised constitution removed all religious restrictions. South Carolina's Protestant state ceased to exist. Catholics and all non-Protestants achieved full citizenship and religious freedom.

North Carolina did not move quite as expeditiously as her more southern neighbors. The constitution of 1776 stated that no church would be established, but limited the legislature to Protestants alone. In a spirit of anti-clericalism, the constitution barred clergymen from holding office. In 1835, an amended constitution allowed any Christian to hold office. Not until 1868 did the state lift all religious tests to office holding and citizenship.

Virginia and Rhode Island alone had full religious freedom when the nation came into being. Tiny Rhode Island had scarcely veered from the teachings of Roger Williams. George Mason's Virginia Bill of Rights had, for all practical purposes, granted religious freedom. Thomas Jefferson's Statutes on Religious Freedom, passed by the Virginia legislature in 1786, made official the religious freedoms of Virginians and completed the de facto disestablishment of the Anglican Church.

The Middle States generally followed the pattern of the

southern. New York provided all but complete religious freedom. A law aimed at Catholics required immigrants to foreswear allegiance to foreign ecclesiastical authority as a requirement for citizenship. In 1806, the state removed even that stipulation.

The New Jersey constitution of 1776 avoided establishing any religion, but favored Protestantism. Under this constitution Catholics had to endure second-class citizenship. Not until 1844 did New Jersey wipe out all religious restrictions to citizenship and office holding.

Pennsylvania, the cradle of American freedom, demonstrated a generous attitude toward all Christians, including Catholics. Jews, however, could be elected to the legislature only after giving allegiance to God and to the Old and New Testaments. In 1790, the oath underwent alteration to allow Jews to hold office simply by giving allegiance to God.

Maryland forsook its openness to all religions in a bitter battle over granting full freedom to Jews. The constitution of 1776 disestablished the Church of England but, in effect, established Christianity as the state's religion. The legislature could impose a tax for the support of the Christian religion. Even worse, however, only those who gave allegiance to Christianity could hold office. Efforts to repeal these repressive provisions failed in 1797, 1801, and 1803. In 1810, the religious tax was repealed but Jews were still denied their civil rights.

A quiet Maryland hero emerged to champion the cause of the Jews. Thomas Kennedy, a state legislator, a Presbyterian layman, purely on principle, on behalf of the approximately one hundred Maryland Jews, assaulted this embarrassing law. From 1818 until 1826, Kennedy battled for repeal. Along the way he received threats, boycott, and electoral defeat. Finally, in 1826, the legislature passed a law repealing the "Jew bill."

Like other states, Delaware had a provision in its 1776 constitution that required all elected officials to take an oath attesting to their belief in Trinitarian Christianity and belief in the Old and New Testaments. The 1792 constitution swept away all religious tests, granting full rights to all citizens, including Jews and Catholics.

New England presents quite another story. With the exception of Rhode Island, New England resisted change. Connecticut, New Hampshire, and Massachusetts clung tenaciously to their religious establishment.

Under the influence of entrenched Congregationalism in Massachusetts, the proposed constitution of 1778 included restrictive religious tests for citizenship and office holding. These provisions were, fortunately, rejected; a freedom of conscience provision took their place. But the Congregationalists did not give up so easily. The ratified constitution allowed the state legislature to require church attendance and proper morality. Church taxes were maintained. The constitution did provide for full freedom for all sects of Christianity, but to hold office one had to foreswear all allegiance to foreign ecclesiastical powers, thus limiting Roman Catholics' religious freedoms.

The Religious Freedom Bill of 1811 took the state further down the road to religious freedom and church/state separation, but not far enough. The Congregationalists and the Unitarians combined forces at an 1820 constitutional convention, beat the Baptists, Methodists, and Quakers, and kept compulsory church attendance on Massachusetts's law books.

But the times were changing—even in Massachusetts. The growing numbers of members in the non-established churches, well-established immigrating Catholics, and the overall impulse toward complete religious freedom forced lawmakers to rethink their attitudes toward church and state. Finally, in 1833, the voters of the state removed all religious tests for citizenship and office-holding. No doubt many Congregationalists in Massachusetts lamented the rising tide of secularism that wiped out their control over the affairs of the state. As a matter of fact, religious tides forced the change. Men and women of the dissenting churches brought about the change, bearing out once again the contention that church/state separation came about because religious people demanded it.

Prior to the Revolutionary War, the people of Connecticut had provided that those who sincerely dissented from the Congregational Church could worship on their own without interference; but they would still have to pay taxes for support of the state church. Changes in 1784 removed language that specifically established the Congregational Church. But dissenters still had to file papers stating their desire to worship on their own. Everyone still had to pay church taxes.

John Leland, a Baptist who moved back and forth between Virginia and New England, decried Connecticut's certificates of dissent and the taxes for the support of religion. But his words fell on deaf ears. Not until 1818 did Connecticut revise its constitution to remove all religious establishments, officially separating church and state and providing full equality before the law to all Christian bodies. This liberality overlooked the few Connecticut Jews and the all-but-nonexistent Muslims and others outside the Christian folds, who only gradually gained their place in the state's sun.

Full religious freedom foundered on New Hampshire's famous granite until the twentieth century. In 1680, the New Hampshire assembly had given civil rights to all English Protestants. Despite flourishing speeches on religious toleration, the New Hampshire constitutional convention of 1783 gratuitously passed articles limiting the offices of governor and legislators to Protestants. William Plumer, another of those unsung heroes of religious liberty, risked his political fortunes to plead against the restrictions. He failed.

Through a grueling bureaucratic process, dissenters from the Congregational churches could, theoretically, secure certificates that would free them from having to pay church taxes, but these papers were exceedingly hard to come by. Baptists, Methodists, and Unitarians need not apply; they almost never escaped the tax collector's clutches. The only alternative was the dankness of a New Hampshire jail.

The election of Thomas Jefferson as President in 1800 brought slight but welcome changes. In 1804, the New Hampshire legislature recognized Baptists as a distinct religious group, thus freeing them from having to pay religious taxes. The Methodists and Unitarians soon gained similar recognition. But the voters of New Hampshire, in spite of the passage of two centuries under the First Amendment, consistently continued to maintain a religious test for office until 1946. What's more, the New Hampshire constitution had, until 1968, an all-but-forgotten provision that allowed towns to levy taxes for the support of the Protestant religion. Certainly Jefferson's wall of separation between church and state had not reached very far into New Hampshire.

Doomsayers in the United States and abroad predicted that religion would collapse, and the nation along with it, unless the state took an active hand in promoting religion. The exact opposite has been the fact. American religion flourished because of the pervasive spirit of freedom and non-interference by government. Up and down the Eastern Seaboard religion expanded. New churches sprang up, especially Baptist, Methodist, and Presbyterian.

As the country grew westward, the various churches responded with missionaries. Circuit-riding preachers became a living part of the history of the growth of this nation. These missionaries, though far from perfect and sometimes imbued with rather narrow theology, brought a sense of morality, justice, and general enlightenment that immeasurably strengthened national foundations.

Religion, in "proper" circles, frequently had an air of gentility. The church member did not get too exercised over his religion. But American religion was not *all* polite and genteel: Prophetic religion, with a cutting edge, played an important role in the United States from the very beginning of our life as a people. The Reverend Alexander McLeod of New York wrote in 1815:

> Ministers have the right of discussing from the pulpit political issues which affect Christian morals. The judicious minister will weigh, in the balance of the sanctuary, every subject, for the purpose of determining its importance. He will rarely enter upon political topics. He will never descend to questions of mere party: but there are times in which he ought not to be silent, respecting the conduct of nations, or of Christians in their civil capacity.[1]

The War of 1812 stirred conflicting sentiments in the nation, including among religious people. Reverend McLeod supported the war. Lyman Beecher opposed it. The war brought into being the nation's first peace groups, whose ongoing influences remain with us still.

Church and state had a significant clash over the government's treatment of the Cherokee Indians in Georgia. Acting under the conditions of a treaty, the Cherokees had settled in a lovely portion of northwest Georgia and had created an admirable civilization. Living in complete peace with their neighbors, the Cherokees developed an alphabet, writings, agriculture, and government. Responding to the Baptist, Methodist, and Presbyterian missionaries who ministered among them, many of the Indians embraced Christianity. When the State of Georgia turned covetous eyes on the Indian territory, Christian men and women came to the defense of the Cherokees. Unfortunately, from President Andrew Jackson to the U.S. Senate to the U.S. Supreme Court, the Cherokees lost out, in spite of the able and devoted work by some U.S. Senators and people in the churches. Exercising their freedom of religion, men and women of deep faith sought to prick the nation's conscience over the treatment of the Indians.

Religious people threw themselves into the various social reform movements that sprang up beginning in the 1820s. American churches, alone and in clusters, addressed problems of urban poverty and temperance, as well as education in the new territories. People of religious commitment tackled problems involved in massive immigration to this nation. Churches and religious communities worked for women's rights and education, militant abolitionism, public education, mental health, and approaches to dealing with America's rapid industrialization.

The presidency of Andrew Jackson had its effect on religious life. An ardent church/state separationist, Jackson dissociated himself from any religious denomination, though he had been reared a Presbyterian. On numerous occasions he made pronouncements that fostered religious liberty and toleration in the new country. In spite of his terrible blind spot when it came to the plight of the Indians, his presidency had a broadening, humanizing influence on American Christianity.

As the nation flowered, churches took on a different character. In the new climate of liberty and freedom from control by government, the churches rapidly developed patterns of self-government, with lay people enjoying ever-increasing roles of responsibility. The churches thrived as free bodies in a free state.

As voluntary associations, subject only to the broadest type of governmental control such as property laws, the churches accepted the principle of church/state separation. Most came to recognize this made-in-America doctrine as one of history's greatest legacies to religious enterprise. Voluntary support for the churches fit in with the American spirit of free enterprise. Stripped of the support of the state in matters of faith, a spirit of cooperation and toleration emerged that strengthened the work and influence of the churches.

The nineteenth century saw the balancing of Protestantism with Roman Catholicism. Waves of immigration from Europe brought Catholics in ever-increasing numbers to the United States. These large numbers fanned latent fears among many Americans that the Pope would effect a takeover of the country. Evoking their English heritage, with its stories of abuses by Rome, colonial Americans had thrown up many barriers to full participation by Catholics. These fears and barriers gave way ever so slowly.

Under the leadership of Father John Carroll, the Holy See in Rome granted American Catholicism a semi-independent status. Father Carroll had demonstrated great skill and unquestioned patriotism during the Revolutionary War, thus allaying the concerns of many about his loyalty to the United States. He had the complete trust of highly placed American leaders, including George Washington. In every way he proved that one could be a devoted follower of the Roman Catholic Church and a faithful American. President Washington eventually showed his appreciation for Bishop Carroll by attending, with cabinet members and other officials, a dinner marking the dedication of St. Peter's Church, the first Roman Catholic church erected in New York City.

A series of Catholic councils, beginning in 1791, charted the course of Catholicism in the United States. These meetings sought to balance traditional church doctrine and practices with the spirit of religious and political freedom in the United States.

Religious peace between Protestants and Catholics, alas, did not endure. The middle decades of the nineteenth century saw far too many nasty outbreaks between the two branches of Christianity. Democracy-loving Americans could not reconcile the absolutism of Catholicism. When fear and prejudice were thrown in, the climate was ripe for trouble.

Catholic theology dealing with the ownership of property and the control of clergy put the church at odds with American society for many years. The Catholic view of trusteeship over property requires that the bishop hold the title to the property. The popular American attitude was that the church was owned by the members, who, through democratic process, should exercise control of its real estate. In Catholic practice, the bishop supervises the clergy. In Protestantism, the lay members of the parish called the pastor, determined his salary, and supervised his work. Frequent conflicts arose within Catholic churches between the congregation and the bishop over the calling or dismissing of the pastor. Protestant members of the community simply could not understand the strange ways of the Catholic church when it came to property and priests.

A frequently virulent Protestant press stirred up strong sentiment against Catholic institutions, especially convents. Horrible stories about life inside the convents flew about the countryside. In an unfortunate 1834 outbreak, a mob burned the Ursuline Convent in Charlestown, Massachusetts, while city fire companies made no move to extinguish the blaze. In response to the violence, the Protestant leaders of Boston issued a joint statement condemning the destruction and decrying the loss of the building but, finally, doing nothing to help restore the property.

Further conflict between Catholicism and the state and American society came as the church gradually, beginning as early as 1782, moved to create a system of parochial schools in which general education could be offered but in a decidedly Roman Catholic context. With Protestantism so dominant, Roman Catholic parents became convinced their children could not receive a balanced education in the public schools. The King James Bible was taught as part of the daily curriculum. In a senseless clash over the use of the Bible in schools, violence erupted in Philadelphia on July 4, 1844, when a riot against the churches of St. Michael and St. Augustine resulted in damage to the property as well as the tragic loss of several lives.

Conflict has existed since the founding of the parochial schools over the use of tax money in those church-sponsored institutions. While the parochial schools have operated with little government interference, most states and the federal government have resisted intense lobbying by Roman Catholics for direct tax support for their institutions. Especially state legislatures have succumbed to parochial-school lobby pressure, finding a multitude of ways to provide indirect support for the schools.

In the middle of the nineteenth century, the Know-Nothing and the Nativist parties rose up in opposition to Catholicism, further intensifying the tension between Catholics and Protestants. Vestiges of these positions remain, and crop up from time to time.

All in all, Catholic Americans, both lay and clergy, have generally demonstrated a capacity to follow the teachings of the Church, maintain a loyalty to the Pope, and still live as faithful and devoted citizens of the United States. The spirit of religious freedom must ever be broadened to embrace those with whom we disagree, even on the outworking of constitutionally guaranteed religious freedom.

Jews came to America as early as 1655, settling primarily in New York but fanning out to other colonies also. The quality of treatment by Jews at the hands of settlers and leaders varied in the colonies. Gradually, over a period of years, American Jews gained both political and religious liberty. At first, the Jews could not have a synagogue. By 1682, however, the Jews of New York had rented a house they could use for worship. By 1695, they were able to own a place of worship.

Jews in colonial America fared best in Massachusetts and South Carolina. The Puritans set aside their innate intolerance when it came to Jews, out of respect for the Jewish prominence in the Old Testament. Early in its history, Harvard University began offering courses in Hebrew. In 1720, an unconverted Jew received a degree from that same institution.

The generous 1669 South Carolina constitution required only that its people have a religion. The second synagogue in America was established in Charleston in 1755. South Carolina sent Francis Salvador, Jr., a Jew, to the First Continental Congress in 1774. Salvador has been described as "the first Jew in American history and probably the first Jew in the modern world to serve in an elective office."[2]

Jews supported the drive for American independence, served in the armies, and gave liberally to the freedom movement. From the first, the Jews, a distinct minority, supported religious freedom. With George Washington setting the example of openness and complete toleration, the Jewish community gradually moved into the mainstream of national life. Under the federal constitution Jews achieved full rights as citizens, but not without some struggle—namely—in Maryland and in North Carolina. As we have seen, discrimination against Jews did not end in Maryland until 1826. North Carolina restricted Jewish political activity until 1868.

Though anti-Semitism seems always to lurk right beneath the surface for some in the United States, Jews have enjoyed their full measure of liberty while still having to deal with an unnecessary amount of prejudice. Certainly they hold high the ideals of religious freedom through their support of the separation of church and state.

Since its earliest days, America had seen itself as something of a fulfillment of biblical prophecy, a concrete realization of the Kingdom of God on earth. A common belief in God that transcended denominational and geographical differences became a vitally important bond that helped give a disparate people a sense of unity and oneness. Just as God had led the Hebrews out of captivity into a new land, so had he led the Americans out of captivity, not just from Great Britain but from old ideas, into the promised land of America and a new way to govern. The Pilgrims on the *Mayflower* described their new home as a "City on a Hill."

The successes the country knew even in its colonial days—victory over the mighty British, the fearless manner in which Americans moved to conquer new territories—played into the religious way in which the country viewed itself. Time and again, the writings and speeches of notable political leaders took on the flavor of sermons reminding the people of their chosenness by God. The pervasiveness of religion contributed to and grew out of this theological consciousness. The sense of divine appointment played itself out in a mixture of genuine humility and haughty arrogance. Americans were the New People chosen by God to take humanity on a giant leap forward. We would be a "nation under God." "In God We Trust" became the national motto that we, ironically and quite un-biblically, placed on our currency.

In our own day, this floating, imprecise, but nonetheless real religious understanding has been labeled "civil religion." America's civil religion has its roots in the Bible—the Jewish and Christian heritage—as well as in the philosophy of the eighteenth-century Enlightenment. De Toqueville picked up this self-perception when he described America as having the soul of a church. He and other European observers commented on the religious nature of American self-understanding.

If one understands what civil religion is and what it is not, then we may safely say that a nation needs a measure of civil religion, a set of commonly held values that tend to bind the country together and give it a clearer vision of itself. To the scholar of the Bible, to the serious theologian, this civil religion poses serious problems. Many expressions of civil religion tend to make the nation self-righteous. It does not foster self-criticism. Civil religion tends to be gratuitous and self-congratulatory. But it is nonetheless important, especially in times of crisis.

The Civil War exploded as the nation's greatest crisis. All the noble aspirations of the Founding Fathers hung in the balance. Would this grand experiment in self-government get blown away in the holocaust of battle? The best and worst of civil religion created part of the climate for the war. Southern religion caved in to the economic forces that depended on slavery. Southern religion extrapolated a theology that defended slavery and, in the process, let slavery define religion. Religion inspired many in the North to rise up against the evils of slavery. The best and worst of national religion emerged, becoming spiritual glue that helped get the country through its terrible bloodbath. Both sides called on God to help. And, in a strange and wonderful way, perhaps he did, even without many Americans living at the time being aware of his providence.

And Abraham Lincoln became the priest of this civil religion. As the conflict broke on the nation, shattering much of the country's self-understanding, calling into grave question its preachings about the ability of a people to govern themselves with order and decency, Lincoln, perhaps alone among national leaders, sought for a higher meaning in the war. In his person the President gathered up the nation's dream, now interrupted if not shattered, of a nation under God. His most enduring contribution may well have been the profound theological understanding he brought to the conflict. He interpreted the War Between the States, the war between brothers, in a manner that laid the foundation for the eventual, if tortured and painfully delayed, reunification. His speeches and writings suggest that the President understood the conflict as God's way of humbling and purifying the nation as well as ridding the country of the moral blight of slavery. Time and again he reminded the nation that God rode above the factional conflict. He was, at the same time, on both sides and on neither side.

To theologians like Horace Bushnell and Philip Schaff, the war was the product of the collective guilt of the nation. Slavery was not the sin of the South alone but of the entire nation. The real issue of the war was whether the nation would in fact become one. Bushnell and Schaff recognized divine judgment in the war but also saw the conflict as a terrible but fortuitous opportunity for renewal and redemption.[3]

A combination of revealed and civil religion carries over to our own day. This muddled but real mix of civil and biblical religion plays an important role in bonding millions of Americans. It also provides the occasion for a good deal of the confusion that exists over the role of government in promoting and using religion.

An examination of church and state in the nineteenth century must include a discussion of Section One of the Fourteenth Amendment to the U.S. Constitution. The applicable section states:

> All persons born or naturalized in the United States, and subject to the jurisdiction thereof, are citizens of the United States and of the State wherein they reside. No State shall make or enforce any law which shall abridge the privileges or immunities of citizens of the United States; nor shall any State deprive any person of life, liberty, or property, without due process of law, nor deny to any person within its jurisdiction the equal protection of the laws.

The Constitution was framed in a climate of controversy between those who wanted a strong central government and those who insisted on states' rights. The intricate balancing of the Constitution reflects efforts by the Founders to accommodate those competing philosophies of national life.

The Bill of Rights, including the Religion Clauses of the First Amendment, which guaranteed religious freedom and the separation of church and state in the eyes of all those involved in its creation, applied only to the national government. Nevertheless, as we have seen, the spirit of the First Amendment rapidly spread to most of the states. Each state dealt internally with its own problems of church and state, which arose only infrequently. In 1833, Chief Justice John Marshall wrote an opinion involving the Bill of Rights, in which he said, "These Amendments contain no expression indicating an intention to apply them to the State governments. This Court cannot so apply them . . ."[4]

The U.S. Supreme Court heard its first actual religious-liberty case in 1845. Ostensibly as a public health measure, the city of New Orleans passed an ordinance making it illegal to expose a dead body, even in church for a funeral. The ordinance was challenged by a citizen who said that his "free exercise" of religion was infringed by the city code.

The U.S. Supreme Court heard the case and declared that

the U.S. Constitution did not have any bearing on the case because the First Amendment affected only the national government. Justice John Catron wrote: "The Constitution of 1789 makes no provision for protecting the citizens of the respective states in their religious liberties; this is left to the state constitutions and laws . . ."[5]

In the aftermath of the Civil War, Congress proposed and the states ratified the Fourteenth Amendment to the Constitution. Its basic intent was to guarantee full freedom and rights of citizenship to former slaves. The amendment extends the guarantees and limitations of the Bill of Rights to the states as well as to the national government, especially the "due process" and "equal protection" clauses.

The gradual evolution of the application of this amendment has been the occasion for endless litigation and debate. It should be noted that changing times and not the U.S. Supreme Court have occasioned the debate. In our present climate of threats to the separation of church and state, those who would like to tear down Mr. Jefferson's "wall" frequently declare that the Fourteenth Amendment was never meant to apply the Bill of Rights to the states, especially in the way the Supreme Court has used it in the last several decades.

As long as the nation was largely Protestant, debates over the relationship between church and state rarely surfaced, especially in the courts. But as the religious makeup of the country has become increasingly diverse, the protections of the First Amendment, channeled through the Fourteenth Amendment, have become central and crucial. It is moot for us to bog down in endless argument over the intent of the Framers and Founders when it comes to applying the Constitution to today's world. The Supreme Court, acting in concert with changing attitudes among the American people, has applied the Bill of Rights to both states *and* national government.

The men and women who created the country in the eighteenth century could not have imagined the complexities of life today. The genius of our system and of the Constitution lies in their ability constantly to gather up our entire history and bring it to bear in dealing with today's problems and opportunities.

Using two hundred years of national history—the collective decisions of our laws and courts—the Supreme Court seeks to apply both the letter *and* substance of the Constitution to issues of church and state, along with all the other matters that come before its august bench.

Part Three

TODAY

CHAPTER NINE

Opening Salvos
of the Present Battle:
Old and New Struggles

Tides that began to swell in the waning years of the nineteenth century set the stage for twentieth-century church/state relations. By the turn of the century, the country was undergoing fundamental changes from at least two sources: immigration and westward expansion. These two powerful forces affected everything about the nation, including the religious makeup and perspective of the people.

At the time of the construction of the U.S. Constitution in 1787, the United States was overwhelmingly Protestant. Pockets of persecuted and misunderstood Roman Catholics lived here and there. A smattering of Jews had made their way to the country but they had little political power, although they were a growing economic force. Events in Europe and a favorable social climate in America created the largest, most rapid mass migration in history.

More than 13 million immigrants came to America between 1865 and 1900, with another nine million pouring in between 1900 and 1910. They came from everywhere, bringing their cultural and religious ways with them. Congregationalist Boston became Roman Catholic Irish. New York became a polyglot international city dotted with ethnic and religious enclaves. Germans and Scandinavians pushed westward to Chicago and beyond. Orientals poured into San Francisco and other parts of the West Coast. As the "huddled masses" flooded into Massachusetts and New York and then scattered out into the country, the prevailing Protestant majority began to feel, at first, subtle, then distinct, pressures.

When an increasingly vigorous Catholic community rubbed shoulders with entrenched Protestants, conflict became inevitable. Fear and prejudice flared on both sides of the Protestant/Catholic fence. The Nativists and Know-Nothings, deeply opposed to the Catholic horde, created embarrassing rumbles that Americans would like to forget. But the concerns were not limited to the narrow-minded and bigoted. Notable Americans like Samuel F. B. Morse, Lyman Beecher, and Horace Bushnell wrote and spoke about the "papist conspiracy" to take over the United States. Responsible leaders saw in the massive immigration a concerted effort by the Holy See to fill up America with Roman Catholics so that the pope could become the dictator.

Unfortunately, the pronouncements of some Catholic authors did not help. Ultra-conservative Catholic writers asked, "Can a Protestant go to heaven?" A list of Protestant "errors" roared through the country, further inflaming passions. To add insult to injury, Pope Leo XIII issued an encyclical letter in 1885 declaring the Pope to have authority over both religious and civil matters. It needs to be said that far-sighted Catholic leaders such as Cardinal James Gibbons, Archbishop John Ireland, and Bishop John J. Keane deplored the attitudes and writings of their fellow religionists. Catholic lay people whose roots went all the way back to the nation's beginnings likewise expressed grave concerns over their "unwashed and untutored" brothers and sisters from Ireland and elsewhere who came flocking to America's shores.

Beyond the vague but real fear of conspiracy, Protestant leaders took exception with the growing Roman Catholic constituency on at least two other points: attitudes toward morality and public education. Late-nineteenth-century Protestantism spent a great deal of its energy maintaining a proper attitude toward the sabbath and fighting alcohol. Catholics, especially the immigrants, seemed to be unbearably lax on these two issues. They tended to keep Sunday in a loose, "Continental" way. And Catholics, especially those of German and Irish descent, certainly consumed a great deal of strong drink with little apparent effort by their clergy to staunch the flow.

Even more damaging, however, were some Catholic leaders' attacks on public education. As we have seen, many Catholic parents had legitimate reasons to object to the pronounced Protestant flavor that prevailed in most public schools. In parts of the country, public schools were little more than state-run Protestant Sunday schools meeting during the week. Outraged Catholic leaders got in trouble with their Protestant neighbors when they decried the public schools as "godless". In a heated religious/political climate, the real issues got lost in the rhetoric. Out of the conflict came the Roman Catholic parochial school system.

The first such school actually opened in 1782 in Philadelphia, but schools did not become part of the official life of the Catholic church until 1829. By 1840, the church operated two hundred parochial schools. Since their beginning, the country has engaged in constant debate over the responsibility of the state to assist in the funding of the church-related schools.

Gradually, however, thanks to Protestant and Catholic men and women of forbearance, understanding, and patriotism, the two distinct views of religion and life found themselves forced to learn to live together. In spite of ongoing and irreconcilable differences, the lives of all Americans are enriched by the presence of both religious traditions.

Traditional Protestants and Roman Catholics were not the only groups experiencing change and development during the latter years of the nineteenth century. Coming from Germany and Scandinavia, Lutherans increased until they became the third-largest Protestant group in the country, after Methodists and Baptists. Eastern Orthodox Church membership swelled to over 100,000 by the turn of the century.

The spirit of religious freedom in the United States provided fertile seedbeds for the proliferation of non-Christian religions and new, uniquely American religious communities. In the waning days of the nineteenth century, Buddhism made its appearance among the Orientals who settled on the West Coast. The Young Men's Buddhist Association was founded in 1898.

Toward the end of the century, more than 500,000 Jews fled the anti-Semitism of the European Continent, especially Eastern Europe, and thus altered the character of traditional American Judaism.

The late nineteenth century witnessed the Mormon phenomenon. These Latter-day Saints sprang up under the leadership of Joseph Smith and Brigham Young. Traditional Protestant denominations subdivided, spawning new groups with their own views of life and religion. Christian Scientists, Jehovah's Witnesses, Theosophists, and many more groups began to claim their own place in the sun.

Women played an important role in the creation of these new communities. Mary Baker Eddy founded Christian Science. Madame Helena Blavatsky, after spending time with Eastern mystics, created The Theosophical Society in New York. Ellen Smith left her stamp forever on Seventh-day Adventists.

Immigration *and* westward expansion shaped American religion and contributed to the discussion of the relationship between church and state. Men and women who rose to the challenge of the unsettled West plunged into the wilderness creating new lives and new religious feelings as they trekked across the mountains and plains. Out on the harsh and unforgiving frontier, traditional religion could quickly get absorbed in the dust of cattle drives and the carnage of Indian wars. This westward expansion further challenged the mainline Protestant hegemony. Committed but often unlettered preachers and missionaries reached out to the West, creating new churches in the process. Denominations that could not adjust quickly to the changing political and religious climate did not have the impact in the West they had enjoyed in the East.

Mixed in with these changing religious mores came increasing complexities in every area of national life, including relations between the church and the state. People in the midst of profound changes can think they are in the grips of sinister drives by evil forces, when, in reality, they are simply struggling to maintain equilibrium on a heaving societal ship. Bottom line: With all the national changes afoot, the familiar ways simply began to give way. To their credit, Protestant, Catholic, Jewish, new and old communities, maneuvered through those wrenching changes with minimal violence and bloodshed. To be sure, we should not get too self-congratulatory. Civilized people ought to manage change without resorting to murder and mayhem. But, as a matter of fact, religious changes have nearly always generated bloodshed. We have had riots—most notably the Philadelphia "Bible" riot of 1844—when angry Protestants attacked Roman Catholics. As unfortunate as such outbursts were, by comparison with other countries experiencing similar changes, the old gave way to the new with relative harmony in the United States, thanks to the pervasive liberal attitude toward religious liberty and our pervasive national commitment to law.

Reflecting the changing religious climate and the ongoing struggle for church and state to relate to each other constructively, early in our national history church and state turned to the courts to help settle differences. In nearly every decision, especially those rendered by the U.S. Supreme Court, the judiciary has shown an appreciation for religion while still making every effort to interpret the U.S. Constitution correctly. A study of these cases also shows an evolution in the decisions of the Supreme Court. Case has built on case, court on court. The Supreme Court has, of necessity, gradually moved from a strict application of the language of the Constitution to an interpretation that, while paying close attention to the original intention of the Framers, takes into account changes in the country and its needs. As we will see, we have a school of legal thinking today represented by conservative lawyers and scholars who say the Supreme Court should stick to the original intention of the Framers. But too much has happened in the United States that could not have possibly been anticipated by the Constitutional Convention of 1787 to make such a literalist approach workable.

A brief sampling of the nineteenth-century church/state Supreme Court cases can give us a flavor of what was happening and serve further to set the stage for twentieth-century developments that have more direct bearing on our lives today. Amazingly enough, Supreme Court decisions, especially in the church/state field, provide interesting reading. It helps to realize that actual people were involved in these cases. Feelings and emotions ran high. Eager lawyers presented their carefully prepared briefs before the bench of the highest court in the land, made up, at least theoretically, of the wisest jurists who could be produced at any given time. Certainly some noble men (and now, woman) have sat on the Court. Of course, we will disagree with some of the decisions even though we impugn the character of the Court to our own individual and national detriment. But we are a people of the law. Much of our strength lies in the fact that we obey the rulings of nine people charged with the awesome responsibility of interpreting the United States Constitution.

Terrett v. Taylor (1815)

In 1776, when Virginia became a state, its legislature passed a law that allowed the Episcopal Church to keep the land and properties it held at that time. In 1801, the legislature changed the law, denied the church its holdings, and rescinded the church's charter as a Virginia corporation.

In 1815, the Supreme Court overturned the 1801 acts by the Virginia legislature. The opinion of the court stated that the state could not deny the members of the church, the religious corporation, the right to hold property.

The case was not decided on First Amendment grounds. Remember, until the Fourteenth Amendment in 1868, the Bill of Rights of the U.S. Constitution did not apply to the individual states. In *Terrett v. Taylor* the Court based its opinion on basic laws that provide protection to all corporations.

Vidal v. Girard's executors (1844)

Stephen Girard of Philadelphia left a large amount of money with the instructions that a school for orphans be established. He wanted all secular subjects taught. But he added a provision that said that "no ecclesiastic, missionary or minister of any sect whatsoever" should ever hold office in the school or even be admitted as a visitor.

Mr. Girard's executors sought to break the will, and hired the eminent Daniel Webster to assist them. In spite of his learned discourse, the Supreme Court refused to overturn the will. Justice Joseph Story, in his opinion, recognized the place of religion in Pennsylvania life but also recognized the right of the late Mr. Girard to insert the "no religion" clause in his bequest.

Permoli v. First Municipality of New Orleans (1845)

We have already mentioned this case, but it needs to be discussed again in the flow of Supreme Court cases dealing with church and state. This was the first "religious liberty" case to reach the U.S. Supreme Court.

In defiance of a New Orleans ordinance banning the display of dead bodies in other than a certain designated parish church, Father Permoli conducted a funeral in which the body of the deceased was displayed in other than the specified church. He refused to the pay the subsequently levied fine, saying that the city ordinance violated his Free Exercise rights under the First Amendment.

The Supreme Court claimed it had no jurisdiction in the case since the First Amendment applied only to the federal government. Father Permoli would have to look to the State of Louisiana and its constitution to protect his religious liberties.

Watson v. Jones (1872)

When the Civil War broke out, Presbyterian churches in Louisville, Kentucky, divided over the issue of slavery. The General Assembly of the Presbyterian Church declared slavery evil and took sides with the Union. The various churches and members in Louisville could not agree. Finally, after the war ended, the question came up as to who owned the properties of churches that had left the denomination.

In a landmark decision, the Supreme Court declared: "The law knows no heresy, and is committed to the support of no dogma, the establishment of no sect," advancing the doctrine of government neutrality toward religion. The decision went on to uphold the American doctrine of religious liberty and the separation of church and state. The court then decided the case by looking at the denominational structure of the General Assembly of the Presbyterian Church. In that structure, the General Assembly was entitled to the property or to decide who got the property. In a church that adhered to strict congregational government, the property would belong to the majority members of the individual organization.

Reynolds v. United States (1878)

Mormons believed in plural marriages. Congress had passed a law prohibiting plural marriages in any territory under its control. George Reynolds, the defendant, asserted that denial of his desire to have plural marriages violated his First Amendment rights.

The Supreme Court upheld Congress's law. In the opinion, the Court rehearsed the formation of the First Amendment. It upheld the Jeffersonian doctrine of the "wall of separation" between church and state. The Court affirmed that Congress has no jurisdiction over belief. But—and here the Court asserted the "compelling state interest" doctrine—Congress can pass laws dealing with behavior that can harm individuals or the state. Mr. Reynolds has the guaranteed freedom to *believe* anything he chooses, but he does not have the freedom to *do* anything he wants to. The state has a compelling interest to maintain order and decency. Acts contrary to the public good come under the jurisdiction of government.

The court also decided two other cases involving Mormons, finding for the state in both, generally using the compelling state-interest doctrine. In each instance, however, the court upheld the idea of religious freedom but said one's religion could not pose a threat to the public order. In these and other similar cases, the Supreme Court has applauded freedom but declared that freedom is not absolute.

(The Supreme Court also used the "compelling state interest" doctrine to decide the *Jacobson v. Massachusetts* case in 1905. The state of Massachusetts could require smallpox vaccination of all residents, even though the shot violated the religious beliefs of an individual.)

Church of the Holy Trinity v. United States (1892)

Holy Trinity Church of New York called an English clergyman to move to America and become the pastor of the congregation. Congress had enacted a law making it illegal to bring in foreigners to perform labor in the United States. Did Congress's law apply to the minister and the church?

The Supreme Court said No. The court looked at the substance of the law, not simply to its language. Congress had not intended for its law to apply in such cases. Furthermore, the court said, to find otherwise would have been to demonstrate hostility to religion. Since the American people are a religious people, such a ruling would be repugnant. Further on in this decision written by Justice David J. Brewer, the justice declared ". . . this is a Christian nation."

In recent years, those who want to remove the "wall of separation" between church and state use the language of this decision. "See, even the Supreme Court says we are a Christian nation."

A closer reading of Justice Brewer's lengthy decision shows that he interpreted Christianity in its broadest meaning. He carefully avoided doctrinal statements, pointing toward a generic Christianity. In subsequent decisions, other courts sought to soften and broaden Justice Brewer's assertion. For instance, a 1908 Court of Appeals decisions declared:

> Our nation and the States composing it are Christian in policy to the extent of embracing and adopting the moral tenets of Christianity as furnishing a sound basis upon which the moral obligations of the citizen to society and the State may be established.

In this case, the Court made a statement about civil religion. A reading of the Bible would let us know quickly that a nation with our wide array of moral failures could not possibly be described as a Christian nation, if by that it is meant, that all the people in the land are and behave like Christians.

Bradfield v. Roberts (1899)

The District of Columbia made a contract with Providence Hospital Corporation by which the District would erect two buildings on the hospital's property that would be used to care for poor citizens of the community. The hospital, though chartered by Congress, was operated by an order of Catholic nuns.

A taxpayer brought suit, alleging an improper mixing of church and state. The Supreme Court upheld the contract, saying that the hospital was a secular institution operated for secular reasons. The beliefs of the officers of the corporation are not material to the nature and function of the institution.

From these nineteenth-century Supreme Court cases one can see that the Court rarely became involved in church/state issues. All in all, as long as the Protestant ethos prevailed in the United States, very few cases even got to the high court. Intense conflicts raged between the various church groups, but they simply did not go to court to settle the disputes or, for sure, the cases did not go to the Supreme Court. As the country has grown and become more diverse, we are infinitely more litigious in every area of life, matters of church and state being no exception.

To sum up church/state cases in the nineteenth century, we can say that the Supreme Court felt it had no jurisdiction in matters of religious liberty arising in the various states. In the Reynolds case, the Court did use the language of the separation of church and state, thus putting to rest the assertion by some today that the modern Supreme Court invented the idea of the separation of church and state.

CHAPTER TEN

Reading, 'Riting, 'Rithmetic, and Religion in the Public Schools

M y elementary and high school education took place in the South, first in Virginia and then in Georgia. Religious activities, especially prayer and Bible reading, were part of the school program in most of the schools I attended. My earliest memories of religion in the school go back to the second grade. About once a week, a pastor from one of the town's churches came and told us stories. Some came straight from the Bible, while others were of a more general nature. Though I remember the man, I recall only one of his stories, but the exposure has stayed with me for all these years.

Of course, I do not remember anyone objecting to these activities; but I was only a child. It probably never occurred to anyone in the community to voice an objection, with the possible exception of some Jewish people who, in that day and time, would have chosen to remain quiet.

My first lesson in "longhand" writing came when the third-grade teacher wrote the Lord's Prayer on the board in cursive and told us to copy it. On a regular basis, in the fifth and sixth grade, we had assembly. Frequently these programs were of a strictly religious nature. I still recall, with some horror, the day in the eighth grade when a revival preacher came to the school and the principal called the entire student body together for a hair-raising, fire-breathing sermon complete with an invitation to renounce our sins and become Christians.

My high school homeroom teacher, the son of a Baptist minister, read the Bible to us every day and led in prayer. Like millions of my fellow students who came along in those simpler times, I thought very little about such practices. On Sunday my family and I usually went to church. Craddock, Virginia, and Clarkston, Georgia, were almost entirely Protestant, and more specifically Baptist, Methodist, and Presbyterian. As an elementary school student, I was not conscious of the religious preferences of my classmates. In our high school in Clarkston, we had at least one family of Roman Catholics. We might also have had a few Jews, though I do not remember any.

My years as pastor of First Baptist Church in Vienna, Georgia, came right after the landmark 1962 and 1963 Supreme Court decisions on prayer and Bible reading. Insulated in the Deep South as we were, those decisions, which caused such a rumble through parts of the nation, caused hardly a ripple in our thinking. The high school principal would let us conduct an assembly program when the evangelist came to town for our annual Baptist revival. That school had no Jews, no Catholics, and no blacks. It was a lily-white Protestant school. The principal, the visiting preacher, and I were, I believe, sensitive enough not to give an invitation to Christian discipleship, but the messages were clearly religious with Baptist approaches to life and religion sprinkled throughout. The principal, one of the great men I have known, would not have dreamed of offending one of his students. I am sure he would gladly have let students miss the assembly if their religious preferences would have required such accommodation. As far as I know, no student asked to be excused.

Atlanta and Calhoun, Georgia, where my wife and I lived during the 1970s had begun to reflect the changing attitudes in the country shaped by the Supreme Court decisions. Atlanta churches made practically no effort to do ministry on public school campuses. The schools had become too religiously and ethnically mixed to think about attempting religious assemblies on the property. Even predominantly Protestant Calhoun began to exert greater caution about religious activities on the school campuses, especially the high school. The principal, a close friend, realized that if he let the visiting preacher at my church address the student body, he would have to let the visiting preachers at other churches have the same privilege. Whereas he could trust my evangelist to be sensitive to changing times, he could not be so sure about other preachers who might want to spend time with his students. I understood his problem. Paradoxically, even though I always looked forward to my visits to the high school during revival week, when the time came that we could no longer go to the schools, no one, as far as I know, missed it. We had never relied on those brief stints to do more than make a quick impression on students, anyway. The other ministers in town and I simply found other ways to work with teenagers.

I did get upset, not so much as a local minister, but as a parent when a child-evangelism professional gained access to one of the elementary schools. The principal, a strong Methodist layman, simply wanted his students to have the benefit of religious instruction—an experience many of the children missed at home. The man who did the teaching certainly meant well, but I took serious exception to his methods and theology and told the principal of my concern. That experience gave me an opportunity to feel the proverbial shoe on the other foot.

My wife, a public school teacher and counselor, and I have frequently debated the role of religion in public schools. She has seen firsthand the emptiness in the lives of so many young people. At the same time, she has experienced the tensions that can quickly arise in a multi-cultured school. One school near the District of Columbia in which she worked had more than thirty distinct cultures represented in its student body. If she had been of a mind to impart generic religion, the mixture of the students would have made it all but impossible.

Our culture has changed. The overwhelming percentage of public high schools have, by necessity, closed their doors to religion. How does a nation that has deep roots in religion and morality impart its ideals to young people, especially in an era when the homes seem to be failing in their teaching roles? As the next step up the training ladder, what kind of responsibility does the public school system have to pass on values and religion?

Frankly, Americans have debated those kinds of questions since public schools first began operation. Beyond imparting knowledge of the basic skills of writing and reading, what do we want our schools to accomplish? What is the role of religious instruction in public schools? How does the separation of church and state play out *vis à vis* public schools?

Early in our history, our leaders began to dream of all American youngsters having the benefit of free public education. With such a vast continent to conquer, with ever-new challenges of self-government, with the Reformation doctrine that everyone should be able to read and interpret the Bible for themselves, it is no wonder colonial Americans early in our history began preliminary movements to provide for public education. But, with such an intense desire that youngsters receive an education, schools and curriculum also became arenas for debate as to the quality and type of education. The direction of this debate varied from one township or colony (or state) to another, as the different areas discussed reflected their own needs and concerns.

The variety of the debate also reflects America's historic commitment to local control of education. From the earliest days of any kind of public education, Americans believed it should be under as much local control as possible. Even today, foreigners cannot understand our commitment to decentralized education. Only recently has the federal government become heavily involved in education. And even with the work of the Department of Education such a presence these days, ultimate control of education still rests with state and local agencies.

Given the American commitment to education and our desire to see values and some kind of religious instruction imparted in public schools, it is no wonder that some of the fiercest battles over the separation of church and state rage in and over religion in the public schools. Many Americans regard the public schools as the only possible avenue for dispensing the common faith or "public piety"[1] that underpins the American Republic. This approach to religion in the public schools is closely akin to Robert Bellah's idea of "civil religion" that we have already talked about. On the other hand, parents, especially those who are members of minority faiths or who claim no religious faith, insist that their children not be subjected to any religious indoctrination or activity in public schools. Conservative political elements make "prayer in public schools" a major plank in their platform. Evangelical writers decry the secular humanism of the public schools. Parochial and other church school leaders make steady runs on the public treasury, seeking to get tax support for their sectarian schools. To get a perspective before we launch into the problems of today, we simply have to do a bit more history.

Public education at public expense for all children is an American invention. Until the 1600s, the church controlled education, determining who attended school and what they studied. Beginning with the Massachusetts School Law of 1647, public schools in America have grown in scope and acceptance. Under the Massachusetts arrangement individual towns were required to conduct schools so that young people could learn to read the Bible and thus prepare themselves to ward off the attacks of Satan. Even though close connections existed in colonial Massachusetts between the religious functions of the townships and the secular functions of the town, the political leaders placed the community's schools under the secular function, the decidedly religious nature of the curriculum notwithstanding. Thus was born the American concept of what became a strong commitment to non-church-related public education. Through the public schools the state could carry out its uncritically accepted, self-assigned task of promoting religion, the state doing the promoting rather than the churches.

As the decades passed, with the change in the religious makeup of Massachusetts and other parts of the country, the heavy emphasis on sectarian education in the public schools began to wane. By 1827, Massachusetts textbook committees were forbidden to purchase books that leaned to any one religious point of view.

In 1837, Massachusetts set up the first board of education in America, electing Horace Mann secretary. As public education became more pervasive in Massachusetts, it also became proportionately less sectarian. Mann insisted that education have a strong moral tone while avoiding sectarian, religious instruction. He and others like him who pioneered public education had a place for the Bible in their schools but religious teachings were to be generic, general in their approach. Certainly no one church could be allowed to gain control of the schools. Horace Mann could hold out against sectarian religious instruction, while accommodating generic religion, because almost everyone in Massachusetts could agree on the broad religious concepts. Remember, in those days of the nineteenth century the country saw itself and was, in fact, Protestant even though that self-understanding faced increasing challenges as other groups, especially Roman Catholics, grew in numbers and political power. Along with the concept of no sectarian instruction in public schools, the idea of no tax money for sectarian schools also gained ever-widening acceptance. By 1855, Massachusetts had a provision forbidding the state from giving any funds to sectarian schools.

The Massachusetts laws greatly curbing religious instruction and emphatically prohibiting funding for church schools were picked up by other states. By about 1850, Connecticut had ceased all denominational instruction in public schools but did retain formal Bible reading, prayers, and hymns as part of the day's opening exercises.

New York, Pennsylvania, and other New England and Middle Atlantic states evolved their own approaches to public education—but nearly always with two caveats: no sectarian instruction and no public funding for church schools. Consistently, framers of state constitutions in the original thirteen and in the new states that came into the Union expressed appreciation for religion and education but went to considerable lengths to keep church and state separate.

Gathering up the prevailing national sentiment, President Ulysses S. Grant made a speech in 1875 in which he lauded public education, insisted that not one tax dollar be spent on church schools, and encouraged families and churches to promote religion. The President concluded his remarks by saying "Keep the Church and State forever separate."[2]

To see how political tides change, the Republican platform of 1876 carried a plank that advocated a constitutional amendment forbidding the use of public money for any sectarian school. Today's Republican Party has dramatically reversed itself on that principle of the separation of church and state.

Twentieth-century state constitutions reflect our past. All require public education and nearly all specifically forbid the use of tax money for sectarian schools. The constitutions likewise almost unanimously forbid sectarian teachings in public schools.

American thinking about public schools has evolved to the point that most people realize that today's public schools must be secular, as opposed to religious, institutions. The country has become too religiously diverse for the schools to function otherwise. With more than three thousand identifiable religious groups in the United States, the task of accommodating all their beliefs in the public schools is impossible. The great tension today arises when attempts are made to maintain the necessary secularity in public schools while avoiding an anti-religious posture. How to talk about the "Creator" to whom Jefferson referred in the Declaration of Independence, how to discuss our religious heritage without becoming sectarian is the task public schools have struggled with for much of this century.

Beginning in the middle of the last century, as we have seen, Roman Catholics solved the problem by simply creating their own parochial school system. In the last twenty years or so, primarily evangelical Christians have addressed the problem by creating thousands of schools that reflect their theological and political views. In both these systems, secular subjects are taught but in line with the particular religious framework of the sponsoring religious communities. Religious instruction and worship are warp and woof of the life of the school. When students enroll in one of these schools, they and their parents fully understand the religious perspective that they will confront. As public schools have come under heavier attack, especially from the New Religious Right, Christian schools have sprung up with greater frequency. Indeed, a Christian school industry is being created as companies come into being to set up and supply the fundamentalist institutions with instructional materials.

Roman Catholic parochial schools have long been represented in Congress and state legislatures by lobbyists, along with public school entities. Today, the Christian schools have established Washington offices to promote their interests with the White House, Congress, and various government agencies.

But the overwhelming majority of parents do not wish to

send their children to private schools and/or cannot afford the tuition and other expenses involved in private education. At the same time, many of these parents express concern about the loss of values in society and want public schools to set about restoring those values. While very few parents and groups advocate denominationally-oriented religious instruction, they do *think* they want some religious practice and indoctrination in the public schools. A recent survey of a sampling of 1,500 Southern Baptists, among history's staunchest supporters of the separation of church and state, showed that 78 percent felt the government should "promote" prayers in public schools. President Reagan never failed to get cheers when he advocated "returning prayers" to the public school classrooms. Many Americans have the vague feeling that something has been lost from the schools when daily prayers ceased to be part of the school program.

This chapter is not designed to discuss educational philosophy, but we have to ask ourselves, "What do we want from our public schools in terms of teaching about morality and religion?" In my youth, growing up in the overwhelmingly Protestant South, teachers, who chose to, could get by with a strong emphasis on religion in the schools. But the South, like the rest of the country, has changed too much for those old practices to continue unchallenged.

I get the feeling that many Americans are groping for some form of "public piety" to be taught in the public schools. We want the schools to impart an amorphous patriotism/religion/motherhood/apple-pie approach to life. Very few want the teachers to give out heavy-handed religious indoctrination. The community would rise up in arms if a public school teacher made a serious attempt to convert a student from one faith to another. Still, politicians make steady references to the golden days when we had prayer and Bible reading. We didn't have drugs and homosexuality then, they seem to say.

Not long ago, I addressed a group of ministers in the South on the subject of separation of church and state as the concept related to public schools. I clearly enunciated my belief that teacher- or school-board-sponsored religious activities have no place on a public school campus. Afterward, one minister came up and said, "I think I understand what you are saying. But if we cannot go onto the high school campus and do evangelism, how do we reach the kids?" He was saying, in effect: If the youngsters are not hemmed up on the campus, we have no other ideas for reaching them for religious commitments.

I had to say, "Surely, you have more imagination than that. It may require more creativity to reach the young people for your church if you do not have the benefit of a semi-captive audience at school. But you can get to the students if you will try. Do not ask the school board to become your partner in evangelism."

What form can religious activities take on a public school campus in the light of prevailing public sentiment and court rulings?

Right off, we need to understand that the school board cannot require any kind of religious activity. I feel no sense of loss in that prohibition. Required religious activities quickly run shallow. Besides, my understanding of religious faith precludes any kind of outside coercion.

Activities such as high school baccalaureate services cannot be required events. When I graduated from Clarkston High School in 1955, we had the baccalaureate in the local Baptist church, with one of the preachers delivering the sermon. We had Christian prayers and hymns. No senior would have thought about missing the event. Baccalaureates, where they are still conducted, are purely voluntary. The last one I attended had little religious content even though several ministers participated. The service was, however, sufficiently inspirational so that the young people could have gone away with a sense of transcendence added to their graduation experience.

In many parts of the country, Christmas Holidays now bear the designation Winter Holidays. To my knowledge no court has ordered such a change in nomenclature. Local school boards, wishing to avoid controversy, have quietly changed the names of such holidays. Some federal courts have spoken out on religious music as part of the public school music program. In most cases the courts have allowed sacred music, especially Christmas music, saying that carols and such have become part of the nation's literature, part of the national heritage, and should not be abandoned simply because of their religious nature. Public school music directors, sensitive to the community's religious diversity, frequently make concerted efforts to use a wide variety of religiously oriented music in their programs. Even then, some parents get irate and want all religious music left out of the school's choral program.

In 1984, the U.S. Congress passed a bill popularly called the "Equal Access" legislation that described the way certain religious activities could take place on some public high school campuses. The bill aimed to allow purely voluntary student religious groups, such as Bible clubs, to meet on public school campuses during non-instructional times. The groups had to be student-initiated. Guests and speakers could be invited to speak to the club, but not with such a regularity as to give the impression that the outsiders sponsored or managed the activity. The school would provide a sponsor in the same way it provided faculty leadership for other clubs on the campus. A further stipulation was that the school had to qualify as a "limited public forum"; that is, the school had to already allow non-curriculum-related clubs to meet on the campus, such as the Chess Club or Key Club, etc.

A broad coalition of First Amendment organizations supported and helped shape the legislation, even though they expressed concerns lest off-campus religious groups use the law as a way to invade the campus with their message. Led by the late John Baker of the Baptist Joint Committee on Public Affairs, the supporting groups labored to come up with a set of guidelines that would satisfy the requirements of the law. Several public school organizations published the guidelines as a way to let their constituents understand the outlines and intentions of the new law.

Of course abuses have occurred, though they do not yet appear to be widespread. The worst offenders are adult leaders of off-campus evangelical student organizations, who want to use the on-campus Bible clubs as a beachhead for their own work among the young people. Many of these student organizations have done commendable work in helping teenagers deal with their problems and providing spiritual guidance.

Problems arise not with *what* the groups do so much as *where* they do their ministry. Campus ministers, in their zeal to help struggling teenagers, can lose sight of the constitutionality and propriety of their work, causing considerable concern from parents of children of minority faiths who do not want their children subjected to religious pressures on the public high school campus. Students themselves can get on a holy crusade to evangelize their school by whatever means they can devise, especially if a charismatic youth leader is on the sidelines cheering them on. This may wreak considerable emotional havoc in a local high school.

The Equal Access issue presents some complications. If the Chess Club or Young Democrats or Republicans have a club at the local high school, why can't the Young Christians or the Young Buddhists? Don't religious youth have free speech and freedom of assembly rights at their high school? Why do school administrators single out religion as the forbidden activity on the campus? To many it seems that religion—once the foundation of American life—has been relegated to the intellectual trash heap.

We have to remember the power of religion to bless and curse. Throughout history, some of humanity's greatest and worst deeds have been done in the name of religion. The Constitution recognizes the unique position of religion by placing it at the top of the list in the Bill of Rights. To exert caution about religious activities on public school campuses is not necessarily to discriminate against religion. To the contrary, frequently the care expressed recognizes the unique place of religion in a person's life. Besides, harried school administrators have enough problems that lie at the heart of their educational assignment. They are understandably reluctant to become referees between the various religious groups who want to influence students. Neither do they want to deal with parents who express deep concern about the kind of religious influence being exerted on their children at school.

Parents and youth leaders who desire a religious club on the high school campus must act with understanding and caution. They must understand the racial, cultural, and religious diversity at most public high schools today. Likewise, religious students and their off-campus leaders must try to appreciate the nearly impossible job laid at the feet of school administrators as they try to satisfy all the clamorings that come their way.

Several court cases have arisen from the Equal Access legislation. While some preliminary rulings have come down, the federal courts have given no definitive statement on the constitutionality of the law. Ultimately, the U.S. Supreme Court will have its say on the law.

For a number of years, parents and educators have expressed serious concerns over the lack of understanding on the part of our youth of the role religion has actually played in our history. In an effort to abide by the First Amendment and, at the same time, to give public school students exposure to the historical importance of religion several groups have made serious attempts to find ways to teach *about* religion in public schools. Even in some of their rulings striking down government-sponsored devotional religious practices in public schools, the Supreme Court has recognized the place of religion in national life and encouraged the schools to develop ways to emphasize our religious heritage. The most substantive, though still not widely used approaches, have come in developing courses on comparative religion and in teaching the Bible as literature.

Some concerned educators created an organization called the National Council for Religion in the Public Schools. This group has developed curriculum materials that public high schools can use, in a constitutional and educationally sound manner, to teach about religion. The materials recognize both the separation of church and state problems on the one hand, and the crying need for education about religion, on the other.

As part of their materials on the Constitutional Bicentennial, the National Archives has developed some excellent material on the Religion Clause of the First Amendment that high school teachers and students can use.

The Americans United Research Foundation has published a book entitled *Religious Liberty in America: A Teacher's Resource Guide*.[3] This publication provides some excellent available material that teachers can use when talking about religious liberty in American history. This foundation also conducts national and area workshops with social studies teachers on how to teach about religious liberty as they work their way through the larger sweep of American history.

In most cases school administrators will work with parents and community leaders in finding acceptable ways to help the school accomplish its educational goals while, at the same time, giving increased attention to the role of religion. Such a task will not be easy, but sensitivity and cooperation all around can go a long way toward achieving laudable ends.

As parents and educators wrestle with the opportunity and problems of teaching about religion in public schools, let me offer the following suggestions in the form of a series of questions and answers:[4]

1. Is it legal to teach about religion in public schools?

Yes. In the Supreme Court rulings (1962 and 1963) against state-sponsored school prayer and Bible reading, the Court stated emphatically that education should include the study of religion. In *Abington v. Schempp*, Justice Tom Clark wrote:

> It might well be said that one's education is not complete without the study of comparative religion or the history of religion and its relation to the advancement of civilization. It certainly may be said that the Bible is worthy of study for its literary and historic qualities. Nothing we have said here indicates that such study of the Bible or religion, when presented objectively as part of a secular program of education, may not be effected consistently with the First Amendment.

2. Is there a summary of what the Supreme Court has held to be legal and illegal in teaching religion in public schools?

The Public Education Religion Studies Center at Wright State University offers these guidelines based on Court rulings:

The school may sponsor the study of religion but may not sponsor the practice of religion.

The school may expose students to all religious views, but may not impose any particular view.

The school's approach to religion is one of instruction, not one of indoctrination.

The function of the school is to educate about all religions, not to convert to any one religion.

The school's approach to religion is academic, not devotional.

The school should study what all people believe, but should not teach a pupil what he or she should believe about religion.

The school should strive for student awareness of all religions, but should not press for student acceptance of any one religion.

3. Why should the study of religion be included in the public school curriculum?

Religions play a central role in human history and society. Therefore, the school curriculum must include the study of religion in order to be accurate and complete. Exclusion of religion gives students the false impression that the religious life of humankind is insignificant or unimportant.

Knowledge of religious issues is also essential if students are to understand religious liberty, the first freedom guaranteed by the Bill of Rights. Moreover, knowledge of the role of religion in history and in the contemporary world can promote understanding between peoples and faiths.

4. Where does religion belong in the curriculum?

Religion should be taught wherever it naturally arises in any subject. On the secondary level, the social studies, literature, and the arts in particular offer many opportunities for the inclusion of religious themes. The elementary curriculum also provides occasions for the natural introduction of religion. Religion belongs in discussions of family, community, different cultures and many other topics discussed in the elementary grades. Integrating the study of religion into existing courses is a natural and educationally sound way to expose a large number of students to the role of religion in human life and history.

Religion may also be taught in special courses or units. Some schools, for example, offer courses such as world religions, the Bible as literature, and the religious literature of the West and East.

5. Is it possible to teach about religion fairly and accurately in the public schools?

The study of religion, like any academic subject, requires adequate teacher preparation and objective, educationally sound teaching materials. Unfortunately, many teacher-training programs and most textbooks seriously neglect religious issues and themes. The situation is improving, however, with the growing demand throughout the country for better treatment of religion in the schools. Already, new teacher-training programs and resources are being developed.

We have not answered such questions as:

What is the relationship between the study of religion and the teaching of values?

In what ways can the biblical account of creation be raised in the public school?

How should religious holidays be treated in the classroom?

What should every high school graduate know about religion?

We have not answered the question "What do we want from our public schools as promoters of morality and religion?" We cannot give quick answers but conscientious school officials, working with concerned, level-headed parents can devise approaches that benefit students and community. Perhaps, at least, now you have a bit more clarity about the dimensions of the problem of dealing with religion in the public schools.

CHAPTER ELEVEN

Forty Years with the Supreme Court, *or* Madalyn Didn't Do It

R arely in American history has one person received so much credit for something she did not do. In the popular mind, Madalyn Murray O'Hair gets all the credit for having prayer and Bible reading taken out of the public schools. And Mrs. O'Hair has done very little to disabuse the public of her minimal role in having required prayers and Bible readings declared unconstitutional. What she has done as a result of the ruling is engage in something of a cottage industry promoting atheism. With her quick mind and bold, slashing tongue, she has tied up many a debater in his own language. She has gifts for gab and headline-grabbing that have brought her considerable media attention. But the net effects of her work are highly over-rated.

Along with bashing Mrs. O'Hair, many citizens engage in the game of Supreme Court bashing, especially for its decisions dealing with religion in public life and in the public schools. In my view, much of the court bashing is misplaced.

During the last forty-plus years, the U.S. Supreme Court rendered a number of important decisions on the constitutional relationship between church and state especially as that principle impacts the educational system. We have to look briefly at some of those cases. In the process, I hope to dispel some of the myths that have grown up and persisted around several of those rulings, particularly the 1962 and 1963 decisions on prayer and Bible reading in the public schools.

Despite what some TV preachers say, church/state cases did not begin with the Supreme Court in the 1940s. As we have already seen, the court began looking at church/state cases as early as 1815. The difference is that, beginning in the 1940s, an unusual number of unusual church/state cases made their way to the Supreme Court. Lest we get too upset at the court for meddling, we need to remind ourselves that courts do not generate lawsuits. American citizens, in conflict, generate cases and go before state and federal courts for resolution.

The Supreme Court did add some new dimensions to church/state lawsuits beginning in the 1940s. For the first time the justices applied the Fourteenth Amendment directly to issues involving the separation of church and state. And, for the first time, the court attempted to define the meaning of the separation of church and state. As we have noted, legal scholars and grumbling politicians will debate the appropriateness of that use of the Fourteenth Amendment for years to come, but that debate lies beyond the scope of this book.

What's more, the Supreme Court generally strengthened the Jeffersonian/Madisonian interpretation of the separation of church and state *not* out of hostility to religion but out of appreciation for religion's role in the lives of the American people. Quite to the contrary, the justices have used their decisions as historical sermons to remind the American people of the vital role that religion has played and of the absolute essentiality of keeping religion free from government interference—and, yes, promotion. At this writing, I have to raise serious fears about the future of religious liberty and the separation of church and state because of the possible shift of the Supreme Court away from a concern about individual liberties to the interests of government and the state. But, at least during recent decades, the court has guarded the wall of separation.

In all the decisions the court based on the First Amendment, they have paid close attention to the two key constitutional phrases: *"no establishment"* of religion and *"free exercise"* of religion (italics are mine). Remember the words of the Religion Clauses of the First Amendment: "Congress shall make no law respecting an establishment of religion or prohibiting the free exercise thereof." Sometimes the case turned on the "no establishment" clause, while others turned on the "free exercise" clause. Most of the cases have been decided on the basis of the "no establishment" clause, the court saying that the net effect of some government action or law was the "establishment" of a religion. These two phrases are central to understanding and deciding church/state cases. Watch for them as we move ahead.

What are those crucial education-related church/state cases that created such a stir in the country? Some are better known than others, but, since decisions build on previous decisions, it will be helpful to look at some of the earlier contests that led up to the pivotal ones in the 1940s.

The voters of Oregon, in a referendum, passed a law making attendance at public schools mandatory. The law was written in such a way as to have the net effect of outlawing private schools. The Supreme Court, in 1925 (*Pierce v. Society of Sisters*), unanimously ruled that Oregon's law was unconstitutional. The Court held that a state can regulate education in its jurisdictions but it cannot require that all education take place in public schools.

In *Cochran v. Louisiana Board of Education* (1930), the court upheld a state law providing textbooks for students enrolled in private parochial schools. Taxpayers upset over the law charged that the money for textbooks imposed an unfair tax on the people for the benefit of the schools. The Supreme Court unanimously upheld the state law. Using the "child benefit" doctrine, the court said the program helped young citizens of Louisiana and not the religious schools. (As an aside, it needs to be said that, as of this writing, Louisiana provides more money per capita for private schools and less for public schools than any state in the nation. Several major lawsuits have been instituted by New Orleans parents challenging this inequity.)

A 1940 case involving members of the Jehovah's Witnesses group, though not directly related to education, does have significance for all future church/state cases. Jesse Cantwell, a member of Jehovah's Witnesses, stopped two New Haven pedestrians on the street and, with their permission, played them a record on a portable phonograph machine. The record criticized other churches, especially Roman Catholics. Police arrested Cantwell for inciting a breach of the peace. He was subsequently convicted of disturbing the peace.

In this case, *Cantwell v. Connecticut* (1940), the Supreme Court reversed the conviction on First Amendment grounds, saying the arrest violated Mr. Cantwell's right to free exercise of religion. The overriding significance of this case is that here, for the first time, the Supreme Court explicitly used the Fourteenth Amendment as the means for extending the First Amendment to the states, though the court had steadily moved in that direction for seventy years.[1] Hereafter, the court used the "Fourteenth for the First" doctrine with regularity.

Two other cases—actually two phases of the same case—growing out of disputes with Jehovah's Witnesses involved religion and the schools. The children of Jehovah's Witness Walter Gobitis refused, on religious grounds, to salute the flag and give the pledge of allegiance. Jehovah's Witnesses believe that saluting the flag gives reverence to a "graven image," thus violating one of the Ten Commandments. The Minersville School District in West Virginia expelled the children. Mr. Gobitis appealed to the federal courts. In 1940, the U.S. Supreme Court (*Minersville School District v. Gobitis*) upheld the expulsion, saying that general laws must be obeyed regardless of problems of religious liberty.

In an astounding yet gratifying reversal, the Supreme Court overturned the Gobitis case in 1943 (*West Virginia State Board of Education v. Barnette*), using the free speech clause rather than the free exercise of religion clause. Participation in patriotic events cannot be made compulsory, the court declared. In some of the court's most eloquent language, Justice Robert H. Jackson wrote:

> If there is any fixed star in our constitutional constellation, it is that no official, high or petty can prescribe what shall be orthodox in politics, nationalism, religion, or other matters of opinion or force citizens to profess by word or act their faith therein. If there are any circumstances which permit an exception, they do not now occur to us.

This broadening of constitutional doctrine set the stage for some earth-shaking decisions involving church and state *vis à vis* public schools.

In *Everson v. Board of Education* (1947), the Supreme Court upheld a New Jersey law providing busing for children attending parochial schools as well as for those going to public schools. The court, picking up on the Cantwell case, elaborated on its belief that the First Amendment's ban against establishing a religion applied to the states because of the Fourteenth Amendment. The court also affirmed that neither the federal government nor a state may aid religion.

The court reasoned that providing the transportation worked for the safety of the children, and only indirectly aided the parochial schools in question. If the state could station police near the schools, it could also provide transportation.

In the *Everson* case, Justice Hugo Black wrote the most definitive statement on the separation of church and state the Court had ever given.

> The "establishment of religion" clause of the First Amendment means at least this: Neither a state nor the Federal Government can set up a church. Neither can pass laws which aid one religion, aid all religions, or prefer one religion over another. . . . No tax . . . can be levied to support any religious activities or institutions, whatever they may be called, or whatever form they may adopt to teach or practice religion . . . In the words of Jefferson, the clause against establishment of religion by law was intended to erect "a wall of separation between church and State."

Is this the application of the First Amendment the framers of the Constitution intended? A reporter from Pat Robertson's Christian Broadcast Network interviewed me recently on the Constitution and religion. He asked, "Do you think the Founding Fathers would approve of the present state of affairs in terms of the Constitution and the Supreme Court's attitude toward religion?"

Good question. Patrick Henry and leaders of his stripe certainly would take exception to the present state of affairs in a wide variety of issues and, yes, to Justice Black's interpretation of the First Amendment. The State of Massachusetts would have taken exception until it finally disestablished the Congregational Church in 1883. Thomas Jefferson, James Madison, George Mason, John Adams, and leaders of their ilk would probably have agreed with the overall interpretation but certainly not in every instance.

Times change. The Constitution stands, but case builds on case, reflecting and shaping the major issues that the American people confront.

In all likelihood the justices who decided the *Everson* case would have admitted that Jefferson's "wall" eluded easy definition. The justices had no notion of expressing an anti-religion sentiment. They simply described a broad principle, the separation of church and state, and then set about to apply it. Ironically, in spite of the powerful separationist language in *Everson*, the court allowed the state to provide bus rides for parochial school children.

On the heels of the *Everson* case, the Supreme Court gave a decision on *McCollum v. Board of Education* (1948). Vashti McCollum, mother of Terry and Jim, took serious objection to a program of religious instruction the Council on Religious Education had worked out with the school administration in Champaign, Illinois.

Under the agreement, once a week, students who wanted to and whose parents had agreed were released from their regular studies for a brief period of religious instruction. The teaching took place *on* the school campuses. The Council on Religious Education supplied the teachers at no charge to the school but subject to final approval by the school administration. Students who did not wish to participate in the religion classes were excused to go to a study hall or otherwise productively engage themselves.

The Supreme Court applied the "no establishment" clause in striking down the Champaign program. By providing space, by working closely with the religious leaders, by promoting the program, the government (the school board, in this instance) violated the First Amendment, in effect establishing a religion.

What was more, the administration's authority to decide who did the teaching presented an opportunity for much mischief and entangling of church and state.

Again, in the *McCollum* case as in the other church/state cases it heard, the Supreme Court made a clear point of saying its ruling in no way expressed a hostility to religion. Such hostility would put the court at odds with American history. "Both religion and government can best work to achieve their lofty aims if each is left free from the other within its respective sphere."

In the 1952 *Zorach v. Clauson* ruling, the court *allowed* students in New York City to leave school property for one hour a week to participate in religious instruction. In effect, the justices said it was unconstitutional for the teaching to take place on school property, with school personnel supervising the program. The Constitution did not suffer if the students *left* the school's premises. Educational authorities could honor the nation's religious heritage by adjusting the school day to allow students to leave public property for religious instruction. Government could make certain "accommodations" to religion without violating the First Amendment, the majority of the court held in this case.

Justices Black, Jackson, and Felix Frankfurter took exception to the court's "accommodationist" theory and wrote strong dissenting opinions. Justice Jackson deplored the "warping" and "twisting" of the "wall of separation" between church and state.

Of all the church/state cases decided by the U.S. Supreme Court in modern times, probably none created an uproar like the 1962 and 1963 rulings on prayer (*Engel v. Vitale*) and Bible reading in public schools (*Schempp v. Abington School District; Murray v. Murray v. Curlett*). Both of these cases have received monumental misreading and misunderstanding by many Americans. I have to suspect that some of the confusion has been deliberately generated by those who want to gain political points by stirring up the public. And, I say again, Madalyn Murray O'Hair, the atheist, played only a minor part in these cases.

In 1951, the New York State Board of Regents, charged with running the state's educational system, recommended that the local public schools begin their day with the following prayer: "Almighty God, we acknowledge our dependence upon Thee, and we beg Thy blessings upon us, our parents, our teachers and our country." A number of local school boards adopted the prayer and made recitation of the prayer a required part of the schools' program.

Right away, the parents of ten pupils in New Hyde Park, most of whom were members of various religious groups in the community, brought suit against the practice, saying that it violated the First Amendment's "no establishment of religion" clause.

The U.S. Supreme Court agreed with the parents, ruling that state government-sponsored school prayer indeed violated that clause of the First Amendment. Justice Black wrote the prevailing opinion; he rejected the state's claim that the prayer was simply part of its program of moral instruction. Black declared that prayer is a part of religion, of religious exercise. The prayer program established the religious beliefs embodied in the prayer. When government attempts to promote, support, establish, or use religion in any way, both church and state suffer. Justice Black went on to say that the founders of our government regarded religion as "too personal, too sacred, too holy, to permit its 'unhallowed perversion' by the civil magistrate." Governmentally established religion and religious persecution go hand in hand. Justice Black insisted that government has no business composing official prayers for any group of Americans. Great danger to liberty comes when the government places "its official stamp of approval upon one particular kind of prayer or one particular form of religious service." The First Amendment stands "as a guarantee that neither the power nor the prestige of the Federal Government would be used to control, support or influence the kinds of prayer the American people can say."

Black declared, as the court had done all along in its rulings on church/state cases, that the decision indicated no hostility toward prayer or religion. "It is neither sacrilegious nor antireligious to say that each separate government in this country should stay out of the business of writing or sanctioning official prayers and leave that purely religious function to the people themselves and to those the people choose to look to for religious guidance."

Justice William O. Douglas, who agreed with the majority, took the occasion of the *Engel* decision to give some profound thoughts on religious freedom. He said:

> The price of religious freedom is double. It is that the church and religion shall live both within and upon that freedom. There cannot be freedom of religion, safeguarded by the state, and intervention by the church or its agencies in the state's domain or dependency on its largess. The great condition of religious liberty is that it be maintained free from sustenance as also from other interferences by the state. For when it comes to rest upon that secular foundation it vanishes with the resting.

Justice Potter Stewart dissented. The prayer program did not violate the Constitution. In his opinion, the justice declared prayer to be part of the national heritage. If children did not pray, they missed out on a major piece of Americana. Justice Stewart, like so many before and after, evinced a utilitarian view of religion. Religion exerts positive good for the state and should, therefore, be encouraged by the state. In all the hullabaloo that followed the *Engel* decision in 1962, many in the country have overlooked the fact that the Supreme Court never even attempted to "outlaw" prayer in public schools. Justice Black and the others who voted with him recognized the complete inability of government to stop anyone from praying whenever the person chooses to pray. In fact, the ruling simply dealt with prescribed prayer and did not mention spontaneous and voluntary praying in public schools.

As a practical matter, the court did not rule out spontaneous, voluntary prayers that teachers or students might feel persuaded to offer at special times. Of course, a student or teacher could not disrupt the class with some kind of aberrant religious outburst, but no court is going to slap a teacher in jail who mentions God or religion or has a moment of prayer for some special reason. In our own time, on January 28, 1986, when the space shuttle *Challenger* exploded, many thousands of students and school officials offered prayers, individually and collectively, for the astronauts and their stricken families. The crucial element in the school-prayer controversy is the role of the government—the school board—in promoting or requiring the religious exercises.

Proponents of school-sponsored prayers say that dissenting youngsters can leave the room during the prayers or simply sit quietly while the class prays. Do you remember when you were seven or eight years old, or even fifteen or sixteen? Did you like to feel estranged from the rest of the class? It is patently unfair to ask children to attend public schools, paid for by the their parents' taxes, and then be made uncomfortable at the most sensitive of all points in one's existence: religion.

Remember how cruel we could be to each other as youngsters? If someone came to school wearing something different or looking different, we could make him or her feel miserable. Teasing, chiding, jeering, even physically attacking our fellow classmates was not unheard of, if they demonstrated sufficient "differentness" from the rest of us. Not in every instance, but in far too many to be permissible, children whose faith did not permit them to participate in the school's established religious exercise had to leave the room, or simply sit in non-participation frequently receiving cruel treatment from their peers. For the dubious benefit of rote prayers, we should not subject youngsters to that kind of pressure—ironically, in the name of religion.

On the heels of the *Engel* decision, school boards and administrators across the country issued their own guidelines, effectively outlawing spoken prayers on their campuses for any reason and under all circumstances. They overreacted out of concern lest their schools become arenas for angry confrontation between pro- and anti-school prayer partisans. School officials overlooked the fact that the court did not forbid individuals praying on campus. The court really did not outlaw occasional, spontaneous prayers in such cases as the crash of the *Challenger*.

How widespread was the practice of school prayer? A survey by Professor R. B. Dierfield of Macalaster College found that, in 1962, only approximately half of American public school districts, mostly in Southern and Eastern states, had some form of mandated prayer.² And even in those parts of the country, that called for religious exercises, the actual practice was spotty.³ Certainly the tradition of opening the school day with prayer, Bible reading, and a pledge to the flag goes back to the earliest days of the common school. But, as we have seen, these exercises quickly took on the garments of civil rather than biblical religion. Many defenders of school prayer stuck up for the devotional time more from a concern for the stability and well-being of the country than out of concern for the spiritual welfare of the youngsters, harking back to the utilitarian view of religion held by many of the country's Founding Fathers.

When the Supreme Court declared state-sponsored religious exercises unconstitutional, many people in the country felt that something basic to the nation's self-understanding went by the board. The hue and cry arose not so much over the loss of prayers as over the shift in the way the nation viewed itself.

To add insult to injury, in *Abington School District v. Schempp; Murray v. Curlett* (1963), the Supreme Court declared unconstitutional required devotional Bible readings in public schools. In deciding the issue, the Supreme Court took two cases dealing with the same subject. Pennsylvania had passed a law requiring that ten verses from the Bible be read without comment every day at the beginning of school. When Edward and Sidney Schempp, Unitarian parents, objected and lodged a lawsuit, federal courts found the Pennsylvania law unconstitutional. In Baltimore, Madalyn Murray and her son William, professed atheists, challenged a 1905 school board regulation that called for Bible reading and a recitation of the Lord's Prayer at the beginning of the school day. The Maryland courts had upheld the practice.

Justice Tom C. Clark wrote the opinion of the court, declaring both the Pennsylvania law and the Baltimore regulation in violation of the "no establishment" clause of the First Amendment, as applied through the Fourteenth Amendment. In his opinion, Justice Clark readily acknowledged that religion has always been a major part of America's self-understanding. But American religion has been sustained not by the state but by individuals and their religious institutions. In implementing religious freedom, the First Amendment, according to Clark (quoting former Wiley B. Justice Rutledge), was designed "to create a complete and permanent separation of the spheres of religious activity and civil authority by comprehensively forbidding every form of public aid or support for religion."

The key qualifiers are "public aid." Neither the public schools nor the public square need be devoid of religion. Religion can grow and flower, but government, in none of its forms, should promote or encourage religion.

In his concurring opinion, Justice William J. Brennan recited the long history of prayer and Bible reading in the public schools, going back to the beginning days of public or common schools. He also recited the long history of controversy over such practices. Brennan wrote that, through the decades, school authorities and state legislatures had wrestled with the problems raised by such obviously Protestant Christian religious activities. Roman Catholics and Jews complained unceasingly of the prayer and Bible reading that violated their own religious sensibilities because Protestant Christian prayers and Bible readings were always used. Thus, Justice Brennan concludes that the U.S. Supreme Court in 1963 did not invent the problem: rather, history finally deposited a festering problem at the High Court's bench.

Some tried to defend prayer and Bible reading as having secular purposes. The court in both instances agreed that school-sponsored religious activities could have secular purposes: building discipline, strengthening moral character, etc. But they insisted that such practices are inherently religious, a fact with which very few proponents disagreed.

A careful reading of the rulings in both the *Engel* and *Schempp* cases fails to turn up a single statement by the Supreme Court *forbidding* prayer and Bible reading in public schools. The court consistently made the point that the state cannot require or sponsor religious activities such as prayer and Bible reading.

Justice Brennan went on to expand on the "neutrality" doctrine. In his view the Religion Clauses of the First Amendment embody neutrality. Following the Constitution, government should maintain an attitude of neutrality toward all religions, neither supporting nor interfering.

As if he anticipated today's arguments about secular humanism, Brennan insisted that neutrality did not mean that government would establish a "religion of secularism." Government cannot prefer one religion over the other—theism vs. atheism, belief over unbelief, monotheism over polytheism. All religions have equal access to the law and stand on an even footing before the bar of justice.

In this opinion, Justice Brennan laid out important parameters for dealing with religion in the public schools. He readily acknowledged that "one's education is not complete without a study of comparative religion or the history of religion and its relationship to the advancement of civilization. It certainly may be said that the Bible is worthy of study for its literary and historic qualities." The discussion in Chapter Ten of methods to teach about religion in public schools, reflects efforts to follow the Supreme Court's advice. Finally, some twenty-five years after the historic decision, education administrators, textbook publishers, and the public are waking up to the constitutional and fair way for Americans to treat religion in tax-supported schools.

To be sure, neither the Regents' prayer nor the required Bible readings represented concerted attempts to establish a religion. But, quoting Madison's *A Memorial and Remonstrance of Religion,* Justice Black cautioned:

> It is proper to take alarm at the first experiment on our liberties . . . Who does not see that the same authority which can establish Christianity in exclusion of all other religions may establish with the same ease any particular sect of Christians, in exclusion of all other sects? That the same authority which can force a citizen to contribute three pence only of his property for the support of any one establishment, may force him to conform to any other establishment in all cases whatsoever?

Why did the decisions on prayer and Bible reading create such an on-going shock wave? The United States, as we have noted in other places, likes to regard itself as a deeply religious nation. Much of this popular religion is a form of civil religion with little biblical or theological content, but still we draw comfort, of sorts, from this fuzzy, amorphous, "God, motherhood and apple pie" feeling. When the Supreme Court demanded the removal of these ingredients of state religion, they struck at something in the national psyche of many Americans. The justices created a *dis*ease in the way we viewed ourselves. Today, even supporters of required prayer and Bible reading concede that the exercises have little or no religious content, but the presence of the rituals support morality and Americanism.

One has to wonder how Old Testament prophets like Jeremiah or Amos would regard such routine religious practices.

Further into this book we will examine some more recent decisions of the Supreme Court dealing with religion in the public schools and in the town square. As long as American religion has vitality, men and women of faith will have to look to the courts to help them settle their disputes over the exact outworkings of religious freedom in everyday life. Be glad we can settle our debates with words and not bullets.

CHAPTER TWELVE

The Once and Future Nation

H istory does not divide itself into neat compartments. Events flow into each other. Oftentimes, history turns important corners and those living in the midst of it all do not understand what has occurred until down the line. With that caveat, and in keeping with common wisdom prevalent today, I want to set the stage for a contemporary discussion of church and state concerns by looking at events in the late sixties and the decade of the seventies.

Under President Reagan, church/state debate has intensified. The reasons for that intensity have tentacles reaching back to the days of our national beginnings but which are immediately traceable to the tumultuous years from about 1963 until 1980— years when nothing would stay nailed down.

In the Deep South, *Brown v. Board of Education* made little immediate impact on ordinary citizens. I was a junior in high school when it came down. At policy-making levels, the ruling may have caused consternation, but at Clarkston, Georgia, near Atlanta, it caused nary a ripple. For all we knew and cared, life would move along as it had. We did not reckon with Martin Luther King, Jr., and all he came to represent. The Supreme Court could issue all the lofty rulings it wanted to. We would manage. But when King began to "stir up communist-inspired trouble" next door in Montgomery, people in the South began to get nervous. Then came the sit-ins at lily-white lunch counters. "Colored" people began to ask themselves, "Why do I have to sit at the back of the bus?" (This was a question I had frequently asked my mother as a boy growing up in Atlanta. With obvious pain she would simply say, "That's just the way it is. It's not right. But that's just the way it is.")

Suddenly the *Pax Eisenhower* began to crumble. Acrid smoke roiled up over city ghettos. The Bull Connors of the country began to rear their ugly heads. Bomb blasts tore away church walls and young lives. Watts. Birmingham. Selma. The March on Washington. Daily, television and the newspapers subjected the nation's sensibilities to a steady barrage of marches, riots, and new demands by black people. The William Sloan Coffins of the country left their comfortable ecclesiastical and academic nests and took to the streets in protest. The Jerry Falwells of the world declared that preachers ought to stay home and save souls.

Perhaps the steady, if profoundly resisted, changes in civil rights paved the way for the election of our first Roman Catholic president. Andrew Young, former UN Ambassador, later Mayor of Atlanta, had a way of saying that the civil rights movement pushed the nation to do what it knew all along to be the just and right way for America to treat its black citizens. If that is the case, and I believe it is, perhaps the changing attitudes toward people of other races eased the country down the political road that enabled them to elect a Catholic. To be sure, Mr. Kennedy barely squeaked into office. But he needed only a one-vote margin and he got that. Sure enough, the Pope in Rome did not try to run the country, at least as far as anyone could tell.

The "pill" as a birth-control device facilitated the sexual revolution. America's youth claimed a new sexual liberation. In my youth, Hollywood movie bedroom scenes always had twin beds. The nation was scandalized when Jane Russell in *The Outlaw* (1949) did a discreet tumble in the hay. As sexual mores loosened, twin beds gave way to double beds. Men and women actually got in bed with each other—fully clothed in pajamas, of course. Then, as the sixties and seventies roared by, violence in movies, always a theme, was joined by sex. We'll never know which comes first: sex in movies and then sex in society, or the reverse. I have an idea they accompanied each other.

In the late sixties, I served as associate pastor of Druid Hills Baptist Church in Atlanta. The senior pastor graciously let me preach fairly often. Once in a Sunday-morning sermon, I mentioned the word "sex." Afterward one of the older ladies, a dear friend and fan, came up to me with a pained look on her face. "Mr. Maddox," she said, "I wish you would not say that word again in our pulpit." When I asked her what word, she nearly choked in saying, "Sex!"

Recently, one pastor made national headlines when he handed out condoms during the Sunday-morning worship service. Indeed, we have changed.

But loose sex created manifold problems. Preachers, especially of the more conservative bent, increasingly began to inveigh against declining morals. Teenage pregnancies began to increase. Divorce became rampant. A creeping uneasiness about the quality of American life began to seep out across the country.

In the early sixties, most of us had hardly heard of Vietnam. We feared the Communist threat around the world; we knew that the Soviet Union was bent on world domination. But we knew we could contain them. We had stalled the Reds in Greece. We had brought about a peace, albeit uneasy, in Korea. As irritating as it was, we could beat the Communists wherever they chose to challenge us. If we had to go to Vietnam—wherever that was—we would just do it.

Looking back on Vietnam, we should have heeded the wise experts who warned us of the folly of fighting in those jungles where friend and foe all look alike, against armies who did not worry about wearing clearly marked uniforms, and with a regime almost as venal as the Communist's. But we did not listen. Instead, with massive doses of national arrogance, we began a devastating trek into awful jungles. The few American technical assistants became a large cadre of advisers. A few dozen soldiers became a few hundred, who became thousands, then hundreds of thousands. Not only did we *not* beat the Communists, we savaged our national soul. We sacrificed more than 55,000 young lives for nothing. The war cost us two presidents. We had to hightail it out of Saigon with the enemy literally at the gates. Only now have we been willing to make blunt movies and write honest books about Vietnam. We gained nothing and lost a great deal.

My wife, young son, and I were riding down the streets of Jacksonville, Florida, on our way to do some early Christmas shopping when news came that President Kennedy had been wounded. We rode on a few minutes, then, with unspoken agreement, turned around and went home. With ineffable sadness and heaviness of spirit we learned of the President's death. I suppose everyone of age at that time can remember where they were when the news broke. This could not be happening in civilized America. Cities burning. People marching in the streets. And now an immensely popular young president struck down.

I will always be in President Kennedy's debt. When he stood up to the Soviets in the Cuban Missile Crisis, I gained a new lease on life as an American. The United States could stem the "Red Tide." Now my president lay dead. Oh, how it hurt!

Then came Robert Kennedy. Then Martin Luther King, Jr., Medgar Evers, and more. Indeed, the subterranean plates of American life were shifting. We did not know who we were anymore.

From 1964 until 1968, I served as pastor of the First Baptist Church, Vienna, Georgia, in Deep South Georgia. Carefully but emphatically, I picked my battles with that wonderful congregation over the racial question. I preached some sermons. We interacted with the black community in a new way. My wife worked in the black school in the first Headstart Program of President Lyndon B. Johnson's Great Society. While I struggled with guilt for not doing more to bring about social change in our town, many of my parishioners worried for me, lest I get in serious trouble with the diehards in the congregation and the community for doing too much.

Along the way during that ministry, I attended a pastors' school at Union Theological Seminary in New York City. The major topic for discussion was abortion. I had never thought seriously about the subject. At that point in time, I don't suppose I had ever known a woman who had had an abortion. In our part of the world, if a young couple got pregnant out of wedlock, they got married. The marriages rarely lasted, but the boy had to do the "right thing" and marry the girl. For the entire week, a variety of scholars debated the ethics, psychology, and sociology of abortion. That New York crowd was light-years ahead of Vienna. The biggest issue in the First Baptist Church, Vienna, Georgia, that summer was where to build the new parsonage. It did not occur to me to come back home and discuss abortion with my congregation.

When the Supreme Court handed down *Roe v. Wade* in 1973, I had become pastor of the First Baptist Church, Calhoun, Georgia. Under Governor Jimmy Carter, Georgia had passed a liberalized but tightly regulated abortion law anticipating the Supreme Court decision. From my work as a pastor, I became aware that young women were having abortions in growing numbers. But we did not deal with the question in our church. I did not *avoid* the subject: It was simply not a topic for conversation, much less preaching.

Not until I joined the White House staff under President Carter and began to deal daily with religious groups—especially the conservative groups—did the full force of the abortion problem hit me. By 1979, for a number of reasons, abortion had become the red-flag issue among the rising tide of what we were beginning to call the New Political and Religious Right.

Totally unprepared, I walked into a meeting of fundamentalist and charismatic leaders at the Rock Church in Virginia, Beach, early in my White House career. Several of them leaped on me with a vengeance because of President Carter's refusal to support an anti-abortion amendment to the U.S. Constitution. It made no difference to these people that the President deeply opposed abortion and had worked constructively to deal with the problem of teenage pregnancies. They wanted him to help them overturn the Supreme Court's decision.

School prayer and abortion have provided the galvanizing elements that pushed strongly conservative religious groups into modern politics. Actually, conservatives never went away. They did generally confine their overtly political activity to such issues as anti-gambling and anti-alcohol and other matters of personal morality, to which more identifiable handles could be affixed. Hunger, peace, economic justice, and other mammoth problems eluded easy management and description, and thus were bypassed by many congregations. Ordinary politics had a tainted air, too secular, so conservatives tended to stay away.

Watergate and the resignation of President Nixon set the stage for the rise of Jimmy Carter. After nearly two decades of wrenching dislocations, the country longed for someone in the White House they could trust. Carter's intelligence, hard work, grassroots beginnings, honesty, and religious faith mixed in with election procedures that worked to his advantage and enabled him to win the presidency over Gerald Ford.

Statistics show that many conservative Christians who were traditionally Republican voted for Jimmy Carter in 1976. One could not say the born-again Christians put him in office, but their votes provided an important edge to his narrow victory.

In the course of the campaign, he described himself as a born-again Christian. Evangelical Christians who come to faith through the experience of a personal decision to believe in and follow Jesus Christ use Jesus' phrase in the Gospel of John about being "born again" as a sort of shorthand to describe their conversion.

Jimmy Carter used the phrase out of a South Georgia Baptist context, a culture that is decidedly "live and let live." South Georgia religion, especially among mainline groups, has a strong measure of grace, forgiveness, forebearance, and open-mindedness toward one's fellow church members. In small-town South Georgia, almost everyone knows who is having an affair, who drinks too much, gambles too much, is presently having financial troubles, and whose children are being especially difficult. Because of ties of family and friendship, such frailties are discounted.

In a more rigid religious community, especially one disconnected from the local geography, "born again" tends to connote a set of social and religious beliefs. In the late seventies, "born again" to millions of conservative Christian believers suggested school prayer, anti-abortion, anti-secular humanism, anti-pornography, etc. When Jimmy Carter refused to ascribe to such an agenda, many of his fellow born-again Christians repudiated him.

Ironically, Carter's born-again-ism worked against him. When Carter, a declared evangelical, became active in politics, a great cloud of his fellows, who had stayed out of active politics, found the permission to jump in. The problem for President Carter came when they all jumped back to their native Republicanism and supported Ronald Reagan.

The cumulative impact of all these changes and dislocations on the nation in general, and on religious sensibilities in particular, created the climate for a social earthquake. Millions in the country began to cast around for a way to manage the upheavals. Even though most Americans understand that our problems are terribly complex, they still want to hear simple answers. We tend to express concern for the future in a longing for a mythical past. In 1979, Jerry Falwell and the Moral Majority, with the help of the highly sophisticated political right, beckoned the country "back to the future."

Jerry Falwell had been in a state of highly agitated political incubation for many years. He founded and shaped, in a fundamentalist mode, the thriving Thomas Road Baptist Church in Lynchburg, Virginia. In the sixties, he numbered himself among the preachers who stayed home and preached the gospel while the liberals marched in Selma. With his folksy, good-old-boy manner, he carved out his own niche on television. As communication technology expanded, he tuned his message to raise more money so that he could reach out to larger and larger television audiences.

In the early fifties, while television was still a black-and-white infant, Oral Roberts and Rex Humbard had learned how to use the airwaves to preach their message and raise large amounts of money in the process. Building on thirty years of experience on radio, Roberts, Humbard, and hundreds more created the "electronic church". A simple, clear, direct message raises more money from passive television audiences, who want to feel religious without doing much about their religion. The television preachers, who are at heart sawdust-trail revival preachers, could match message and medium to communicate with large numbers of Americans.

The National Religious Broadcasters, an auxiliary of the National Association of Evangelicals, gathered up this growing brood of radio and television preachers. Under the able leadership of Union Theological Seminary—trained Dr. Ben Armstrong, this growing army of Christian communicators came to the self-understanding that they had considerable religious and political clout.

It is difficult to say exactly when the media preachers turned overtly political. Reflecting their religious culture, they had always defined sin almost exclusively in terms of drinking, loose sex, divorce, and generally wild living. Being, naturally, politically and theologically conservative, the religious airwaves carried a heavy dose of anti-Communism and super-nationalism— approached in simplistic terms. They hatched out conspiracies with regularity, such as the boogie man Tri-Lateral Commission fear of the mid-seventies, which, surprisingly enough, still lingers in the minds of many good people who get most of their public affairs information from Christian radio stations.

To their credit, Oral Roberts, Rex Humbard, Billy Graham, and Robert Schuller, the granddaddies of religious television, have stayed clear of politics except to make occasional prophetic pronouncements with political overtones. Graham has managed to minister to several presidents, both Republican and Democratic.

By 1979, many in the evangelical media ministry had adopted the New Political Right agenda. The very preachers who had complained about their colleagues who went to Selma now felt called to enter the political lists to reclaim America's heritage. So, the portion of the media dubbed by the rest of the media New Right and Religious Right came thundering out of the canyons of society to rescue America from herself.

The most political of the big-name television preachers are Jerry Falwell and Pat Robertson. Interestingly enough, they have kept their distance from each other even though they both live in Virginia and both are arch-conservative Republicans. Rarely do they appear on the same platform together. Robertson delivers a more astute conservative message. Falwell has maintained his down-home approach. As leader of the Moral Majority, Falwell has become the most visible of the new breed of television preachers. *He* is the one to get, anytime the national media wants a commentary on the present moral and religious scene.

The three most damaging preachers, when it comes to confusing the church/state scene, are Pat Robertson, Jimmy Swaggart, from Baton Rouge, Louisiana, and James Kennedy from Fort Lauderdale, Florida. These men take great delight in denigrating the honored principle of the separation of church and state. Their historical renderings make a historian's skin crawl as they romp through American history prooftexting the Founding Fathers and reshaping events to undergird their point that the separation of church and state is a satanic ploy hatched by the modern-day Supreme Court.

What is the political agenda of this new wave?

Their flag issues are anti-abortion, returning God to the public school classroom, public funding for religious schools, militarism, no treaties with the Soviet Union, laissez-faire economics—to name only the more obvious. Their real agenda seems to be to impose greater control over the private lives of American citizens in order to bring more social stability to the nation. When Robertson and Kennedy slash the separation of church and state so vigorously, one begins to puzzle whether, in fact, they do not want some kind of official state religion. They certainly do advocate a close organic alliance between government and religion, especially the present Republican Party/New Right brand.

Ronald Reagan has the uncontested crown as the worst president in American history on the separation of church and state. With apparently little regard for our history, ignoring the religious pluralism of the country, Mr. Reagan advocated state-sponsored school prayer. In a disregard for two hundred years of American history that precludes tax support for religious schools, he urged Congress to find new ways to fund sectarian institutions. He overturned a century of tradition based on good history and constitutional law by appointing an ambassador to the Roman Catholic Church. Mr. Reagan, has blessed far-reaching efforts to rewrite American history in an effort to blur the protective line of separation between church and state. He has appointed judges who may well cast his destructive influence far into the future.

Mr. Reagan is actually an evangelist for civil religion. His deep love for America, mixed in with the history-less approach to his presidency, prompt him to fuzz important distinctions on many issues, including religious freedom and church/state separation. One writer has described his political theology as a sort of civic club mixture: the pledge to the flag, a tossed-off prayer, roast beef, a rousing speech, then back to the "real" world.

President Reagan will remain an enigma. Most Americans have come to realize he had little in-depth knowledge of what he talked about. His hands-off management style became apparent during the Iran/contra disturbance, but he managed to retain the affection of the country. Even many longtime church/state activists never picked up in his speeches the danger to religious liberty. As I traveled the country during his golden years, people who had labored long and hard for the principles of separation were surprised to hear my criticisms of the President's views on the subject.

In short, the waves of unsettling events and changes that have cascaded over the nation have made us terribly uneasy. In such times of uncertainty, we tend to look around for people and ideas to help us manage our heaving society. Millions of concerned Americans do not want this country to go down in moral and spiritual defeat. Many bought the message of the television preachers when they declared that, if only we did not have the separation of church and state our problems would not be so severe. When a highly respected religious leader like Bill Bright of Campus Crusade for Christ traced the fall of American youth from the Supreme Court's decision disallowing official prayers, people listened, and in their eagerness to find answers accepted such a simplistic approach.

We must take alarm lest in an effort to maintain order in the country, we sacrifice our freedoms. We look back on a mythologized past. We think we long for a return to those simpler days. They were not simple. The country had monumental problems in defining itself, in dealing with slavery, with the Indians, with the robber barons, with wars and depressions. We think American society was more homogeneous in the last century than in this one, but even that is a myth.

Millions of people from Europe came pouring into the country looking for a fresh start. The country experienced great stress in dealing with those masses. We think we remember simple days in schools, when the day began with prayer, Bible reading, and a resounding pledge to the flag. We think we remember the days when America was indeed the "city on a hill" beckoning to the world's "tired and poor." In fact, many people sought to extinguish that light, to close the doors. We had great struggles. The only way to deal with today is to deal with today. Certainly we need to be fully informed about our past as a guide for today and for the future. But no one yet has mastered the technology to turn back the clock. We have an incredible measure of freedom, especially religious freedom. We should not let a president or a television preacher or a manipulative historian persuade us that glorious, uncomplicated days of yore existed when, in fact, they did not.

CHAPTER THIRTEEN

Today's Problems

The end of the decade, the end of the century loom. What are the besetting problems in church/state relations? What kind of dangers lurk for this cherished freedom, the right to retain control of our beliefs and the religious practices that spring from what we believe?

An overarching, persistent problem in every era with any freedom is the lack of understanding that can erode a basic right. When public officials undercut the principle of the separation of church and state, they lay the axe to the root of religious freedom. When, for the sake of conformity, or to achieve a greater degree of homogeneity in our society, we ask the government to support and encourage religion, we have admitted our individual failure to nurture a basic freedom. When we ask government to write and lead prayers in public schools, we have admitted massive failure in our homes and faith communities. When we ask government to fund our religious schools, we say that individual religious groups lack the will to fund their own educational enterprises. To be sure, excesses have occurred in the name of the separation of church and state. Part of my task in this book is to help correct inequities. But let us correct the mistakes, and provide clarity and balance, without abandoning the principle.

Today's specific church/state problems are vexing and myriad. As we wade off into the swirling waters of present-day situations, we have to keep in mind the basic benchmark for evaluation, the Religion Clauses of the First Amendment, with their two thrusts: government cannot make a law establishing a religion nor can it interfere with the free exercise of religion. A basic tool for deciding given church/state situations, in the light of the First Amendment, is to look at the role of government.

Two major Supreme Court cases govern the specific applications of the Religion Clauses of the First Amendment. The *Lemon v. Kurtzman* case relates to the Establishment Clause. The *Sherbert v. Verner* case impacts the application of the Free Exercise clause.

Let me explain:

In *Lemon v. Kurtzman* (1971), the then-Chief Justice of the U.S. Supreme Court, Warren Burger, drew up a test for government actions *vis à vis* their relationship to the Establishment Clause in church and state issues. The case involved a plan advanced by the Pennsylvania legislature to aid parochial schools: To pass constitutional muster, a government action must

(1) have a secular purpose as opposed to a religious purpose;
(2) not involve excessive entanglement in religion;
(3) not advance or interfere with religion.

The court ruled that if a government action failed any one of the prongs of the test, the entire action was unconstitutional.

Sherbert v. Verner involved a member of the Seventh-day Adventist Church. When religious convictions prevented the church member from working on Saturdays, she was fired from her job. When she applied for unemployment compensation, the state refused to pay. The Supreme Court upheld the church member saying the state had infringed her free exercise of religion. In this case, the court developed a test for determining the constitutionality of state action in a free exercise situation. The Court said the government must show a "compelling state interest" in overriding a free exercise claim. The Court also said that a free exercise right could be overridden only if the state could not find "a less restrictive means" for carrying out its function.

Indeed, these tests by the Supreme Court have become the most significant tools for determining constitutionality in church/

state cases. From time to time in this section dealing with today's problems, we will refer to the Lemon and the Sherbert tests.

Parochiaid

Parochiaid is a shorthand way of talking about the entire question of tax support for sectarian education, especially church-related elementary and secondary education. In other chapters we have mentioned this problem. Now I want to discuss the issue in more detail.

Of the several persistent church/state conflicts, this one has lingered for nearly two hundred years. Certainly since the time when Roman Catholic parishes and religious orders began making significant commitments to education, state legislatures and the U.S. Congress have heard a steady drumbeat clamoring for tax support. Parochiaid forces have worked especially hard since the close of World War II, their efforts having met with notable success, especially at the state level.

What is the basic problem in providing tax support for religious schools? Such support violates the "no Establishment" clause of the U.S. Constitution. When government funds the schools with tax money, it is supporting and establishing the religion underlying and being taught through the school. If the school so secularizes and sanitizes its curriculum that it can get tax money, its basic reason for existence—namely, general education in a particular religious context—gets lost in the shuffle. If a Catholic school ceases to be Catholic just to qualify for public support, it could better close its doors and let leaders, teachers, and parents channel their energies in ways that would more faithfully mirror the basic dedications of their faith.

Beyond the constitutional question, we must reckon with the matter of ownership of the schools. As a general rule of thumb, public tax money must be used in places where the administration of the funds can be controlled. Churches rightfully own their own schools. Just as churches should not be subject to state control other than for safety regulations, neither should the day schools they operate. The schools' asking for unregulated money violates good public policy. To accept the money and invite regulations undercuts the mission of the church and is a violation of the "free exercise" clause of the U.S. Constitution.

Indeed, the entire issue of tax support for church schools poses a classic *Catch-22* situation.

Sectarian school leaders argue they should receive tax money because of the nature of their service to the public. Roman Catholic parents, in particular, complain because of the double taxation they face: taxes for public schools their children do not attend and tuition payments to the parochial schools they do attend. Our tax laws are confusing enough without slicing them up further to accommodate religious groups who want money for their schools.

More than two hundred years of public policy in America dictates that tax money should be only used for public schools. Part of James Madison's fight with Patrick Henry in the Virginia legislature in 1785 was an attempt to ensure that tax money did not fund religious education. The essence of Madison's philosophy of the separation of church and state and no public funding for religious enterprises found its way into the First Amendment. As early as 1818, the State of Connecticut included language in its constitution that strictly limited education tax money to the public or commons schools. Since then, most of the states have laws or constitutions forbidding or dramatically limiting the use of tax money for sectarian education.

One of the first big fights over the use of tax money for Roman Catholic schools came in the 1840s when New York Archbishop John Hughes actively sought tax support for the church's schools. Some in the church went so far as to put together a Roman Catholic ticket for state elections. Reacting to the pressure, the New York legislature passed a tight, clear law prohibiting the use of tax money for any sectarian school.

How times have changed. Through the intervening decades, the New York legislature has caved in to sectarian schools' lobbies time and again. Though exact figures are hard to compile, experts estimate that the State of New York now provides approximately $158 million a year, through a variety of programs, to hundreds of sectarian schools.[1]

Recently a group of citizens in Syracuse, New York, became incensed when they discovered an unrestricted $100,000 grant in the state budget to a small girls' day school in their city run by a religious order. Upon investigation, they discovered that two local state legislators, whose daughters attended the school, had inserted the grant in the budget under a New York provision that allows members of the legislature to insert special items.

The Syracuse group organized themselves and have now lodged a lawsuit challenging that grant. A federal judge has put a temporary hold on the grant until the issue is settled. Further investigation of the New York state budget revealed hundreds of thousands of dollars earmarked by members of the legislature for a wide variety of religious programs including activities in sectarian schools.

The 1842 action by the New York legislature precipitated similar action in many other states to cease funding sectarian schools. Prior to the New York controversy, several Eastern states had regularly given grants to Protestant and Catholic institutions. By the outbreak of the Civil War, most states had rewritten their state constitutions, prohibiting public funding for any sort of religious activity, including sectarian schools.

Admittedly, part of this rush of sentiment in the middle of the nineteenth century arose in reaction to the waves of Roman Catholic immigrants from Europe. State legislatures, it could be said, in some instances, "Did the right thing for the wrong reason."[2] Across the ensuing decades, many in places of leadership have come to recognize the value of the sectarian schools to the overall education of many American youth. This new appreciation, however, should not blind political leaders to the importance of sustaining long-standing public policy and its strong constitutional foundations. Public money must go to public schools. Religious groups have every right to maintain their schools, but they should not look to public tax money for support.

Some church groups with significant commitments to education do not seek tax money. The widespread network of Seventh-day Adventist schools comes to mind. The various American conferences of Seventh-day Adventists provide over 1,000 primary and secondary schools attended by approximately 50,000 students. This denomination takes no public money at all. In fact, American Seventh-day Adventists run away from any kind of tax money, lest the various government agencies attempt to exert control over the schools. The denomination and the parents, at considerable sacrifice, pay their own bills.

One of the unfortunate new wrinkles in the battle for tax money for religious schools has come from the rise of evangelical schools. Undeniably, part of the drive by conservative religious groups to blur the line of separation between church and state comes in an attempt to build a case for tax funding for these rapidly growing institutions. Conservative historical revisionists cite such documents as the North West Ordinance of 1787, which encourages the propagation of religion in the new territories. They quote George Washington and other Founders as they extol the importance of religion to American life as justification for seeking tax money from state legislatures and Congress. Indeed, the threat to the separation of church and state today is intensified as Roman Catholic and Christian school advocates join forces to demand public support for educational institutions.

Schools that seek tax money for their operations fall victim to short-sighted planning. Suppose they secure even more funding for their schools and become increasingly dependent on the public dole for their operations. What happens when tax money regulators begin exercising greater control over the internal operations of the schools? What happens when new state and national administrations, and public sentiment, turn against the funding? Schools that have become dependent on the tax money will surely suffer. If the government does its job, it must monitor how taxes are used. Schools, public and private, already stagger under a load of regulations and requirements. Why invite even more scrutiny? Why face the prospect of hiring even more auditors and internal control officers just to keep up with the tax money the school receives? If the school cannot carry its own weight, the demands of the market dictate that it close. The American system of free enterprise mandates nothing less.

Heartless? Not at all. American inventiveness will find a way to educate young people. If a church school closes, public schools have wide-open doors. If one church school closes, another one cannot be too far away. One has to suspect that sectarian schools can build up a voraciously money-hungry, self-perpetuating bureaucracy—just like government. The American public has a hard enough time feeding government bureaucracies. Taxpayers should not be asked to feed church bureaucracies, even those with laudable aims.

Roman Catholic parochial school leaders have made the search for tax dollars a matter of policy. One cannot accuse them of subterfuge. They openly seek the money; they lobby legislatures, Congress, and government agencies for support. Those who would resist efforts by parochial school lobbies need only read literature produced by the sectarian school lobbyists to know where they intend to go. The program calls for steady assaults on government at every level.

So far, the states and the Congress have resisted efforts to provide direct aid to the parochial schools. The courts have allowed a host of indirect contributions. We have cited the *Everson* case of 1947, in which the Supreme Court allowed states to pay for transportation to and from parochial schools. Some forty years down the pike from that decision, the public has gradually become acquainted with some gross abuses of that accommodation. For instance, in some parts of New Orleans public school children must meet their buses at 6:30 A.M., so that the same buses can then make another run and pick up parochial school children. For reasons that elude us, public and parochial school children cannot ride on the same bus, even though the route may go right by both schools.

New Orleans taxpayers have filed a lawsuit against this and other practices. In the discovery process of preparing the case, lawyers for the taxpayers have uncovered a school bus driver organization, almost like a union, that has abused the intent of the *Everson* ruling. In other instances, parents of sectarian school children get paid to drive their own children to school. Documents in other communities show that the public pays thousands of dollars a year to hire taxis to transport children several miles, even outside their home county, so they can attend a sectarian school.

Courts have allowed tax dollars to provide computers for training purposes in sectarian schools. Now it becomes apparent that some sectarian schools have made use of the computers not only to train students in their use, but to use the machines to maintain internal records. In some instances, the sponsoring churches have taken over the use of the tax-provided machines to keep their own records. Some would say, "Look, the machine just sits there for hours, not in use. Why can't the school or the church use it. No harm comes to the computer. It saves the school and the church money."

Remember what I said earlier about monitoring. The computers have a dedicated purpose—only for instruction. The schools accept the machines with that clear understanding. To use the computers for other than their prescribed purpose is to: (1) break the law, and (2) invite government regulators to come snooping into the internal affairs of the institution. The message to the sectarian schools is clear: Either use the machine according to the law or buy your own.

In 1965, as part of his Great Society legislation, President Johnson persuaded Congress to pass a massive education bill (Elementary and Secondary School Act of 1965); it had some highly commendable aspects but was flawed on the point of separation of church and state.[3] Behind-the-scenes maneuvering convinced the President that he had to trade with the parochial school lobbies in order to get the entire bill passed. The $1.2 billion act injected the federal government into education funding in new, far more substantial ways with far-reaching impact on public and private education. Under the Chapter I (Title I) portion of the act, Congress provided funds for remedial education for disadvantaged children in all schools, including sectarian institutions. Many church/state separationists opposed this portion of the bill, while other staunch separationists were persuaded to support it.

The outworking of the legislation allowed public school teachers at public expense to go onto the campuses of sectarian schools for the purpose of providing the remedial education. Almost immediately, advocates of religious liberty began to decry the use of the funds on parochial school premises. Lawsuits were shaped that would challenge the constitutionality of that aspect of the program.

To accommodate the letter and spirit of the act, which contained some First Amendment language, some rather bizarre approaches were made. In one community in Kansas City, a local parochial school began receiving the teacher support for youngsters who had fallen behind in basic skills. Federal regulators visited the parochial school to monitor the effectiveness of the program. Upon entering the classroom where the school teacher worked, the regulator noticed religious symbols on the walls and in other places in the room. Immediately, the government agent informed the principal of the parochial school that the symbols would have to go. The room would have to be sanitized of all religious symbols because the education was taking place under the aegis of the government and government could not establish religion.

The principal indignantly objected. The symbols would stay. Well, then, the regulator informed the principal, the teacher would not. When word of the conflict drifted up the parochial school bureaucracy, the order was issued: Strip the room of all religious symbols. As I warned, in order to get the money the religious mission of the school suffered.

Come now. Surely they could have left a small crucifix hanging on the wall. What's the harm! As we have said over and over in this book, the Constitution clearly forbids any law establishing a religion. In today's highly pluralistic country, the cross in a room whose teacher and supplies come from the public treasury does not pass muster of the Constitution or of fair play. The government cannot be seen as fostering religion, even in a subtle manner.

Missouri's state constitution has a strict prohibition against the use of tax money for parochial education—so strict, in fact, that advocates of accepting federal money for remedial education had to devise a legal way around the limitation. The parochiaid supporters came up with a bypass program. They created an organization through which the money was channeled— laundered, in today's political vernacular. In effect, the tax money went to the secular organization, which in turn hired the remedial education teachers and sent them to the parochial schools.

Dr. Hugh Wamble, a historian and theologian in Kansas City, began building a record for a federal lawsuit challenging Chapter I in his city. Jay Wabeke and Albert Dilley began working for a similar end but along different lines in Grand Rapids, Michigan. The Public Education and Religious Liberty (PEARL) organization in New York City, independent of other similar efforts, also challenged Chapter I as it applied in that city. All three cases began working their way up through the federal judicial system—a long, tedious, and terribly expensive process.

In 1984, the U.S. Supreme Court agreed to hear the Grand Rapids case (*Grand Rapids School District v. Ball*) and the New York case (*Aguilard v. Felton*) as companions; that is, they would hear arguments on both at the same time. Finally, on July 1, 1985, the Supreme Court in effect said that public funding of remedial education *on the premises* of parochial schools violated the U.S. Constitution. The Supreme Court agreed that Congress had the right to provide the funds for the programs and that all children who needed the instruction should receive it. But the programs had to take place on neutral sites. The decisions on Grand Rapids and New York had the net effect of deciding the Kansas City case also. The Supreme Court had struck another blow for religious freedom and the separation of church and state.

The decision caused great consternation in both public and parochial schools. Public schools faced a problem because the original legislation placed the burden for administering the remedial education program on them. How could they accommodate the Supreme Court's rulings in time for the opening of school, only a few weeks away? Sectarian schools faced a problem because they wanted to receive the benefits of the program. They had children who needed the special attention.

With a great measure of American inventiveness, the sectarian school interests set about finding ways to get what they wanted. By 1985, the parochial school lobby had a new ally in the person of the recently appointed Secretary of the U.S. Department of Education, Dr. William Bennett. Bennett, well trained, capable, himself a product of Roman Catholic parochial schools, thoroughly committed to the Reagan agenda of providing tax support for parochial schools, apparently set out to find ways to thwart the rulings of the Supreme Court. To "speed" him along the path of compliance, Americans United for Separation of Church and State lodged a cluster of lawsuits against the secretary even seeking to make him personally liable for costly delays.

In almost every case, the parochial school administrators have avoided transporting the Chapter I eligible students to neutral sites, such as nearby public schools or other public buildings. They have seized on the idea of mobile classrooms—often rather elaborate vans—that would park on the streets adjacent to the parochial school campus. Inside the vans, the publicly paid teachers would provide the important remedial education. At this writing, one education bill under consideration in Congress would provide $30 million for mobile classrooms and vans.

In other instances, sectarian school officials persuaded public school boards that such places as church recreation halls and choir rooms met the prescribed standard for neutrality. In their determination to have it their way, sectarian school officials have badgered public school boards, have in many places refused to cooperate, and/or have insisted on the terribly expensive method of purchasing fleets of tailor-made vans that can park at the curb.

As you can imagine, these attempts to twist the Supreme Court's rulings for the advantage of the private schools have spawned fresh lawsuits. A group of public school parents in San Francisco has lodged a lawsuit designed to test the constitutionality of the attempts to get around the court's ruling.

Supporters of parochiaid have come up with two methods for securing public financial support for sectarian schools: variations on tuition tax credits/deductions and tuition vouchers.

Senators Packwood and Moynihan, both supporters of some form of parochiaid, introduced into the U.S. Congress a bill allowing parents of sectarian school children to take a tuition tax credit off their federal income tax. The allowable credit would reduce one's tax liability by that amount. The House of Representatives approved the bill but the Senate rejected it, so the initiative died. Another scheme is tuition tax deduction. This program would allow a certain deduction from one's federal income tax such as a charitable contribution or medical expenses. This bill, though introduced in several ways, has never made any headway in the U.S. Congress.

The State of Minnesota passed a tuition tax credit bill that the Supreme Court upheld because it, in theory, applied to parents with children in school, private or public. A recent report published by the Minnesota Tax Study Commission recommended that the program cease, thereby restoring approximately $7.4 million in lost income for the state. Naturally, lobbyists for parochial and private schools vowed to pull out all the stops to keep the deduction program alive. The net effect is that the taxpayers of Minnesota are subsidizing private education by approximately $7 million a year through the deductions program alone.

Variations on a voucher program continue to come before legislatures and the U.S. Congress. The voucher idea first came into vogue in the 1950s, but it has actually never caught on. The voucher would serve as a "check" from the government that a parent could "cash" at any private school. Secretary of Education William Bennett has tried unsuccessfully on two occasions to get the Congress interested in such a program. Bennett touted his proposal as "revenue neutral"; that is, existing money would simply get shifted around to the voucher program. Of course, we all know that no government program is ever "revenue neutral." In hearings before a House Education sub-committee in 1986, even members of Mr. Bennett's own party turned thumbs down on the idea.

California and New Hampshire ran pilot programs for vouchers in limited areas of their states for a brief time. The approach proved unsatisfactory, costly, and did not make any significant difference in the enrollments of the various schools, so the pilot efforts ceased. At this writing, no state has a voucher program, though several have one under consideration.

Do the American people want tax support for religious schools? In the last twenty years, voters in twelve states and the District of Columbia have rejected parochiaid fifteen times. Only once, in South Dakota in 1986, did the voters approve the initiative. In November 1986, the people of Massachusetts, a heavily Roman Catholic state, defeated a proposed constitutional amendment permitting more parochiaid by 70 to 30 percent.

Will state lawmakers and parochiaid lobbyists take the hint? Probably not. During one recent legislative season, at least seven states had some form of parochiaid bill under consideration.

Roman Catholic parochial school officials have vowed never to relent in their efforts to secure public funding for their schools. They have a nationwide organization that spends considerable time and money on their efforts. If one could total up the public contribution to sectarian education that already exists, it would be staggering. For the sake of the Constitution, for the sake of public education, and finally for the sake of the private schools themselves, church/state separationists must continue to encourage "friendly" lawmakers to resist the intense pressures they experience from proponents of parochiaid. The parochiaid people have history on their side. They are a dedicated lot who just keep chipping away at public opinion and lawmakers. All their efforts must meet with careful, well-organized resistance.

U.S. Diplomatic Recognition of the Vatican

I never cease to be amazed at what a popular president can do, especially if his timing is right. President Ronald Reagan slid through legislation permitting him to establish diplomatic ties with the Roman Catholic Church, when others before him had failed. An immensely charismatic Pope to whom Mr. Reagan would send the ambassador only served to grease the legislative skids.

As early as 1797, the United States had a consular representation at the Vatican, though he did not have ambassadorial status. From the earliest days of independence, leaders in the new government of the United States had tossed around the idea of a representative. John Adams thought such recognition to be a deplorable idea and in 1779 so informed the Continental Congress. In those days, the Pope controlled a considerable territory in Italy known as the Papal States. A political as well as ecclesiastical entity existed, to which a duly appointed commissioner could be sent. Today, the actual territory of the Vatican consists of 108 acres in the heart of the city of Rome.

In 1846, a man of great appeal to Americans won elevation to the Chair of Peter. Any remaining hesitation that lingered in the minds of American leaders over the appointment of a

full representative to the Vatican disappeared amidst enthu-
siastic outpourings for the newly elected Pius IX. President
James K. Polk nominated as ambassador Jacob L. Martin, a
former Protestant who had converted to Roman Catholicism.
In instructing Mr. Martin in his duties, Secretary of State James
Buchanan urged him to stay out of church affairs. The secretary
charged Martin to cultivate friendly relations with the Vatican
and to increase trade between the two nations.

The diplomatic relationship lasted until 1867, when Congress
refused to appropriate any more money for the Vatican lega-
tion. The twenty years had had their rough spots: Pope Pius
IX wrote letters to President Jefferson Davis of the Confederacy
as well as to President Abraham Lincoln. The Pope's Davis
correspondence angered many in the North and stirred up
anxieties that the Vatican might recognize the Confederacy.
The thorniest problems of all came, however, over the problem of Protestant worship within the walls of Rome. In those
days, when the Pope had complete power over the Papal States,
including the city of Rome, Protestant worship was not allowed. Only after considerable maneuvering was the American
ambassador able to work it out for Protestants to worship. Finally, in exasperation over all the problems—especially the
Pope's perceived dalliance with the Confederacy and the problem of worship—the U.S. Congress simply let the relationship
drop.

Interestingly enough, the Papal States did not send *their* representative to Washington during the entire twenty years.

Not until World War II did the issue of diplomatic ties with
the Vatican again come up. In 1939, President Franklin D.
Roosevelt sent Myron C. Taylor to the Vatican as his personal
representative to Pope Pius XII. Most of the leaders of the
American Protestant community rose up in arms about the
appointment. The President brought some of the leaders into
the White House to soothe their feathers, but concerns persisted. The envoy remained in Rome throughout the war and
even into Harry S. Truman's presidency.

On several occasions, religious leaders called on President
Truman asking him to withdraw Taylor. The President kept

assuring them that the envoy would remain in Rome only long enough to facilitate the peace.

Apparently all along, Mr. Truman had intended to establish full diplomatic ties with the Vatican. To the surprise and un-mitigated fury of the entire Protestant religious community, President Truman announced in October 1951 that he in-tended to create full ties with the Vatican and appoint General Mark W. Clark as ambassador. From every corner of the nation a storm of protest arose. Protestant Americans roared their disapproval in rallies, speeches, editorials, denunciations, hundreds of thousands of letters all livid at the prospect of the U.S. government's recognizing a religion with full diplomatic representation. After three months of this hail of protest, the general requested that his name be withdrawn. The President agreed. He threatened to nominate another ambassador, but did not.

Presidents Eisenhower, Kennedy, and Johnson made no move to send an envoy. In 1970, President Nixon surprised the nation by appointing Henry Cabot Lodge, his 1960 running mate, as his personal representative to the Vatican. Presidents Ford and Carter also sent personal representatives to the Vatican. Mr. Reagan named his friend William Wilson to the spot when he came into office in 1981.

In the summer of 1983, Clement J. Zablocki, a veteran Wis-consin Congressman, introduced legislation which, if passed, would clear the way for President Reagan to establish diplomatic ties with the Holy See. In those days, Mr. Reagan met very little resistance on anything he undertook. With the U.S. Senate in the hands of Republicans who unfailingly did the President's bidding, the legislative way quickly opened for him to extend full diplomatic recognition to the Roman Catholic Church. As in the days in 1847, when President Polk sent his representative, a popular pope and a popular president overwhelmed the Constitution. Once the Vatican ball began to roll, no one could stop it.

This time around, unfortunately, massive public opposition simply never materialized. Times had changed. The Roman Catholic Church, especially in America, had put on a new face of toleration and acceptance of those outside its faith. For decades, in the spirit of ecumenism, Protestant, Catholic, and Jewish faith groups had tried to work together for the common good, seeking to establish harmony and understanding, thus making those who had objections more reluctant to mount vigorous protests. The President got his way.

To be sure, nearly every major Protestant religious group voiced concerns. At the confirmation hearings for Mr. Wilson, whom the President had nominated—the first real opportunity the opponents had to testify before the Congress—all the reasons were advanced why the nomination should not proceed. For once, North Carolina's ultra-conservative Senator Jesse Helms agreed with the church/state separationists and voted, as a matter of principle, not to confirm Wilson. But the confirmation was never in doubt. It passed 81 to 13.

After the appointment, Americans United for Separation of Church and State assembled a broad array of Protestant, Jewish, and even Catholic plaintiffs and filed a lawsuit in federal district court seeking to have the appointment declared unconstitutional. Probably no other church/state lawsuit ever filed in the United States encompassed such a broad spectrum of theological opinion. After much labor and careful argument on the part of the plaintiffs, the federal district judge threw the case out of court on the technical grounds of standing: The group lacked the proper credentials, the legal standing, to bring a lawsuit of this nature. The judge never focused on the merits of the case; he did not consider the constitutionality of the appointment. The lawsuit met a similar fate at the appeals level and never gained entry to the U.S. Supreme Court. So the appointment stands, for now. The only available remedy is for Congress to defend the embassy at the Vatican or for a future president to choose not to reappoint.

What is the problem? Why not have an ambassador to the Holy See? Are we not, as the Reagan Administration contended, sending an ambassador to the Vatican City State? The Vatican ambassador can avail himself of the worldwide network of "listeners" that the Holy See's diplomatic corps has in place.

The U.S. Constitution says that Congress can make no laws establishing a religion. An appointment of an ambassador to a church violates the "establishment" clause.

The Roman Catholic Church does not even see itself as a political entity. In a speech in 1984, Archbishop Pio Laghi, the papal *pronuncio* (ambassador) to the United States, admitted that the United States had not recognized the tiny piece of ground called Vatican City. Rather, we had recognized the Holy Father in his mission as the Vicar of Christ.[4] Anyway one looks at it, the U.S. government has sent an ambassador to a church.

In the *Everson* case, the Supreme Court declared that the government cannot prefer one religion over another. Clearly, the U.S. government has chosen to single out the Roman Catholic Church and the Pope to receive special treatment. What if the Baptist World Alliance or the World Council of Churches or the World Evangelical Fellowship set up diplomatic corps? Would the United States send ambassadors to those institutions? I hardly think so.

It is true that the Constitution gives the president the responsibility for the conduct of foreign policy. But he still must act within the Constitution. The separation of powers does not mean that a federal judge can never question any action of a president as he conducts foreign policy.

President Roosevelt worked, through his personal envoy Myron C. Taylor, to attempt to influence the selection of some key bishops who, the President surmised, would look with favor on his administration. Mr. Wilson, as ambassador to the Holy See, embarrassed the country and the President. He became involved in a portion of the Vatican Bank scandal. He failed to go through proper channels in his work. Worst of all, he tried to conduct secret conversations with Libya. Finally, the State Department, with support from the White House, persuaded him to retire and return to his native California, where he could stay out of harm's way.

It will be interesting to see America's reaction to the relationship when the church has a pope not as popular as John Paul II and an administration whose president lacks Mr. Reagan's charm. Perhaps only time will repair this constitutional inequity. In the meantime, several national groups have begun building a file to support future initiatives to correct this injustice.

Churches, Preachers, and Politics

Churches (let me use "churches" as shorthand for all religious groups) and, by extension, religious people and clergy have played active roles in politics and public affairs since the earliest days of the nation. Their involvement in shaping public policy, even in electing candidates, is simply part of the history of the nation.

In other parts of this book we have noted the churches' political activities in such issues as independence, framing the Constitution, and battling slavery. As a prelude to talking about religion and politics today, let us spend a few minutes rehearsing the history of religious involvement in public policy since the Civil War.

After the Civil War, major Protestant churches turned their attention to lobbying for Prohibition (seeking to impede the sale and distribution of alcoholic beverages), the abolition of prostitution, the censorship of allegedly indecent entertainment, and the retention of Protestant values in public schools. Episcopalians and Lutherans showed much less enthusiasm about these matters of personal morality than some of the more evangelical denominations. Baptists, Presbyterians, and especially Methodists eagerly entered the lists against these moral evils. The Roman Catholic Church remained decidedly non-political, concerning itself more with its own agenda, such as the development of the parochial school system and dealing with millions of immigrants many of whom belonged to the church. More liberal Protestants like the Congregationalists and Unitarians focused their energies on the reform of such problems as child labor laws, inadequate housing, venal business barons, and other social issues. Jewish groups, like the Catholics, had their own agenda, primarily immigration and a concern about the persecution of fellow Jews overseas.

After a national Prohibition amendment was added to the U.S. Constitution in 1919, the victorious evangelicals now sought Bible-reading and school prayer laws, anti-evolution statutes (eventually passed in nine Southern states), and restrictions on immigration from Catholic, Jewish, and Eastern Orthodox countries.

Because of the relative weakness of the federal government prior to the coming of President Roosevelt's New Deal, most church political activity occurred at the state and local levels. However, at the end of World War I, the nation's then two largest religious bodies, the Catholics and the Methodists, opened large Washington offices in order to monitor and influence national legislation.

The Catholic bishops' statements at that time anticipated New Deal social legislation, calling as they did for some form of social security, unemployment insurance, and other social welfare measures.

In the 1940s, several other religious groups established Washington offices as the federal government became more complex and influential. Nine Baptist denominations created what became the Baptist Joint Committee on Public Affairs. The National Council of Churches also began to emerge as a shaper of public policy. To provide a conservative counterbalance to the National Council of Churches, the National Association of Evangelicals came into existence and set up a public affairs office in Washington.

The most pronounced thrust of organized religious/political activity in Washington, however, has come since Lyndon Johnson's Great Society programs began to involve religious groups in a variety of ways. The civil rights movement and opposition to the Vietnam War also fueled church political activity. Then, as we have noted, a backlash against a changing society in the late 1970s brought a renewed lobby of conservative evangelicals to the nation's capital.

Today, approximately seventy-five religious lobbies, or groups that have a religious character, work in Washington seeking to influence the executive, legislative, and judicial arms of government and, by extension, the labyrinthine bureaucracy these government branches have spawned.

As problems bearing on personal and social morality, the family, and education—to name only a few—intensify, religious groups will surely remain a political force to be reckoned with. The Constitution does not forbid such political activity. In fact, the First Amendment basically reigns in government as it deals with religion rather than attempting to control religious activity. This large measure of religious freedom, however, should not be taken as a license for religious groups to act with indifference and arrogance in the political arena. Serious potential pitfalls *vis à vis* churches and politics demand our attention.

Religious groups themselves face the danger of becoming so politicized, particularly along party lines, that they will take on the coloration of a secular political-action committee and be regarded as such by members of Congress and state legislatures.[5] Thus, they will be courted, used, and, surely, abused by politicians. When the various religious groups cannot deliver the votes of their members back home, they will be seen by many politicians as nuisances to be tolerated. The great danger is that religious groups may become politically sagacious but spiritually irrelevant.

The continued politicizing of religion threatens the internal vitality of the churches and certainly dislocates the basic priorities of the American religious community. Any group that has profound pronouncements on *everything* soon is noticed by no one. Church leadership, or bureaucracy, cannot get too far out of step with the membership or its people will become alienated and begin to drift away from the denomination. For years, the "gathering storm in the churches" that sociologist Jeffrey Hadden discerned in 1968 has become a raging fire.[6] For example: The Catholic bishops' pastoral letters on war and peace, and on the economy, have provoked thoughtful but firm rejection from conservative and Republican-leaning Catholic voters and officeholders.

Despite the nearly unanimous rejection of Reagan Administration politics by the Washington spokespersons of the leading mainline Protestant denominations, voters, identified as mainline Protestants, gave 65 percent of their votes to Reagan in 1984 thus rejecting the leadership of their public affairs officers.

The religious lobbying question poses some severe difficulties. The basic problem here revolves around the church's tax-exempt status. Free speech guarantees in the First Amendment grant churches the right to speak out on and act for legislation and candidates as they choose. Internal Revenue regulations, however, allow the Service to lift the tax-exempt status of any 501(c)(3) organization that becomes too political. Non-profit, tax-exempt organizations cannot have it both ways: They cannot enjoy tax advantages and unbridled political activity at the same time. In defense of the Internal Revenue Service, it generally leans over backward to avoid lifting tax-exempt status. But once the exemption is lifted, it is exceedingly difficult to get it back.

As we noted in Chapter Two, a major court case presently working its way up the judicial ladder may clear up some ambiguities. The case revolves around a challenge by the Abortion Rights Mobilization organization's charge that Roman Catholic bishops have violated their tax-exempt status because of their activity on behalf of candidates for public office who hold an anti-abortion position. Abortion Rights Mobilization has actually sued the Internal Revenue Service because it has *not* lifted the tax-exempt status of the Catholic Bishops' Conference.

The concerns expressed in this case have already created an air of caution among church lobbyists. The Roman Catholic Archbishop of Detroit has warned his parishes to take great care in gathering signatures for a new anti-abortion campaign. The Baptist Joint Committee on Public Affairs has challenged the IRS's plans to tighten its rules on permissible lobbying activities.

Another unresolved question asks whether church-owned newspapers can endorse candidates or publish voting records or positions of candidates on issues of vital concern to their religious constituency. For example, Texas's *Baptist Standard* published candidate responses on the issue of gambling before the 1986 elections. The paper has a long history of opposition to state lotteries and pari-mutuel betting. Several Catholic diocesan newspapers routinely publish candidate responses to a wide variety of issues. Whether this activity would cause churches to lose their tax exemption remains uncertain. Until these questions are resolved legally, church groups do well to proceed with caution, lest their political enthusiasms become counterproductive.

At this point a primer, if you please, on church political

activity might prove instructive. Not many of the Do's and Don'ts are set in concrete. In every instance, out of concern for their tax-exempt status, churches should engage in political activity with caution, but, even more so, out of concern for their own ministry and the overall well-being of the political process. When churches decide to act politically, they must see red flags of caution on every corner. Just because churches *can* act politically does not mean they *should*. Any reading of American history, especially the era that gave us our national independence and U.S. Constitution, shows how uneasy the Founding Fathers were with heavy-handed political activity by the churches. Probably Jefferson, Madison, and a few others like them lay awake at night worrying lest religious freedom lead to political divisions within the country.

The church should look to its own polity in deciding to act politically. Who runs the church? The congregation, an executive board, the pastor? In our day of intense scrutiny by regulatory agencies, the press, and the public, a church should not simply drift off into political activity. In the days of Protestant hegemony, the local Baptist or Methodist church could act with virtual impunity, but those days no longer exist.

Clearly, churches may take some actions without offending the Constitution or the Internal Revenue Service. Among them are the following:

Churches may encourage voter registration and may allow church facilities to be used by duly constituted voter registrars.

Churches may establish voter-information forums and may invite candidates to appear for question-and-answer sessions. These should be nonpartisan and not designed to benefit any political candidate or party.

A list of church members may be provided to candidates for use in seeking support for raising funds, but only if it is made available to other individuals and organizations. If a charge is normally made for the list, each candidate should pay the same amount. No favoritism should be shown among candidates in providing a list of congregation members. As a matter of general practice, providing this list of members to any candidate should probably be avoided.

A church may give its mailing list to a legislative organization on the same basis that the list is made available to other organizations. If a legislative organization is given more favorable terms for receiving a mailing list than other organizations, the cost of the list would be considered a legislative expenditure.

What about pastors of individual congregations? In general:

A pastor may personally endorse candidates for public office. Depending on the individual church structure, a potential danger exists in such endorsements. If the pastor is seen as speaking *for* the church, his endorsement could raise serious questions about the tax exemption. Free speech allows ministers to express themselves politically. The Internal Revenue Service has the right to examine the tax-exempt status of the congregation when such endorsements occur. In every instance the minister must weigh the prudence of an endorsement or political stand that might provoke controversy in the church or larger community.

A minister may allow a candidate to use his name as a supporter or to list him in political advertisements.

A minister may engage in lobbying activities in his individual capacity without adversely affecting the tax-exempt status of his church. The minister should be careful not to seek the official endorsement of the congregation in such lobbying activity, lest the tax exemption of the church come under investigation.

Ministers and other like-minded citizens may establish a political action committee, but the committee should exist as a separate entity from the church. Creation of a PAC would seem more appropriate for a referendum or issue campaign than for a candidate or partisan election.

Clearly churches may *not* engage in the following political activities and retain their tax-exempt status:

Churches may not endorse candidates for political office and ministers may not endorse candidates on behalf of their congregations.

Churches may not establish political action committees.

Churches may not engage in "substantial" (as distinguished from electoral) legislative activity. The substantiality of legislative activities usually is measured by reference to church expenditures. As a general rule of thumb, expenditures of under five percent of an organization's total budget are not considered substantial.

From these lists one can see that churches can do more than they cannot. Many questions fall into the twilight zone. The church must struggle with its own ministry and its witness in a community as it contemplates political actions.

In my view:

A candidate should not be allowed to appeal to a congregation at a church service for support of funds to be used in a political campaign.

Since Article VI of our federal Constitution unequivocally forbids the imposition of religious tests for public office, candidates should not be supported or endorsed solely because of their religious affiliation. While this admonition has suffered repeated violations in American history, it bears repeating today.

Churches should not attempt to gain subsidies for their institutions or pet projects from the general tax fund whose monies come from taxpayers of a wide variety of belief of unbelief. Churches who constantly seek sectarian advantage or parochial interest create mistrust and interfaith tension. The cause of religion and civil harmony suffer when churches, especially those with political clout in a given community, bully lawmakers into supporting this or that project.

Churches should not seek to impose their distinctive dogmas on the general population, or to see their theological doctrines imbedded in the civil law. To this point, we do well to heed the helpful advice of the eminent American Protestant theologian John C. Bennett in his 1958 book *Christians and the State*:

> The churches in America should not use their members as political pressure groups to get special ecclesiastical privileges for themselves as against other religious bodies. They should not seek legislation . . . which interferes with the religious liberty of minorities and they should be thankful that the courts stand guard at this point.
>
> No church, no matter how powerful, should bring pres-

sure on the state to enact laws which are based upon principles that depend for their validity on its own doctrine or
ethos . . . It is wrong to seek to make the ethos of one part
of the community the basis of law.[7]

Churches and ministers should not encourage sectarian bloc
voting. Nothing disrupts communal peace and harmony in society like political division along religious lines. The mobilization of religious voting blocs directly threatens the sensible
principles of a pluralistic democracy.

A variation of the bloc-voting threat is the apparent attempt
of some religious enthusiasts to dictate to members of Congress
how they must vote on issues. If a member fails to vote the
proper way, the religious pressure groups frequently label the
lawmaker as un-Christian, immoral, or worse.

The bottom line: Religious citizens abuse the political process
at great peril to church and state.

Religious liberty is a right in the Constitution. Practices growing out of a set of beliefs are always open to examination by
society and the courts. Religious citizens can undercut their
privileges in society if they, in the eyes of that society, overstep
the bounds of decency.

Religious groups can so misuse the political system that the
very state which supports their freedom suffers and even falls.

Religion and Public Schools

We have talked at some length about prayer and Bible reading in the public schools. At this writing, no serious attempts
to alter public policy on these issues are moving around in
Congress or in the states. We looked at the concept of Equal
Access and concluded that, so far, the 1984 law has not caused
much trouble either way. We have seen no surging efforts to
establish religious clubs on high school campuses because of
the law. I hasten to say that the problems of religion and the
public schools persist. As I gaze in my crystal ball, I predict no
end to the debate. As long as the Republic stands, and we have
both religion and public schools, questions will arise.

We do need to look at the following areas of concern *vis à
vis* the separation of church and state that present themselves

today: textbooks, creationism, values education, and the assault on public education by conservative extremists.

In 1986, federal district judges in Tennessee and Alabama handed down decisions involving public school textbooks as they related to religion or the religious views of students. The Tennessee case, *Mozert v. Hawkins County Board of Education*, came about when parents with children in the public schools of Hawkins County, Tennessee, requested that their children be excused from having to study the Holt, Reinhart Reading Series. The parents cited numerous instances in the series that, they alleged, taught the religion of secular humanism. They especially objected to the feminist, "anti-family," anti-God teachings they saw in the textbooks.

When the parents first raised their objections, principals in the schools that their children attended arranged for alternative reading programs. When the matter came before the county school board, the members ruled that the students would have to study the series or face disciplinary action.

As so often happens in such disruptions, feelings began to run high. Before too long, the parents had been briefly arrested for trespassing on school property, the children expelled from schools, and another church/state lawsuit had begun its tortuous way through the federal courts.

Two arch-rivals backed the two sides, rolled up their sleeves, and prepared to do legal battle. Norman Lear's People for the American Way backed the school board, providing most of the costs for legal counsel. Beverly LaHaye's Concerned Women for America paid the legal bills for the parents. The case fell in the lap of U.S. District Judge Thomas G. Hull. At first, the judge refused to hear the case. The parents appealed to the Circuit Court of Appeals, which, in turn, ordered Judge Hull to conduct a trial on the merits of the case. A lengthy trial ensued, followed closely by the media—who dubbed the proceedings "Scopes II." Many distortions of the facts filtered out through news reports that can be straightened out only by reading an incredibly voluminous trial record.

After careful deliberation, Judge Hull handed down his ruling. In part, using the Sherbert test, he decided that the parents' "free exercise" of religion had suffered because of the text-books. The judge did not say the books taught secular human-ism, only that the parents felt they did; and that was all that mattered at that point of law.

But, the judge said, to remove the textbooks from the cur-riculum or to allow the children to read an alternative line of books would, in effect, violate the "no establishment" clause because the school would be establishing the fundamentalist reli-gious views of the parents. Therefore, when reading time came each day, the children could leave the room and have their parents or some designee of the parents teach them reading.

By the time the trial took place and the judge reached his decision, the children had left the public schools and had begun to study in a private Christian school. Since the school board had expelled the children because of their religious beliefs, Judge Hull awarded the plaintiffs $50,521 in compensation for having to pay tuition in the private school.

Concerned Women for America tried to claim complete vin-dication for their fundamentalist views, which is a distortion of what happened—they won part of the case but lost other points. People for the American Way issued an emergency fund-raising letter, saying the decision sounded the death knell for public schools. This was also a distortion of the facts and the judge's decision.

Groups such as Americans United for Separation of Church and State and the Baptist Joint Committee for Public Affairs issued statements lamenting the whole sordid mess, expressing concern for the future of public education if that kind of caf-eteria hopscotch mentality caught on, but saying that the judge's decision relating to the Religion Clauses was true to the First Amendment.

Counsel for the school board promptly appealed the decision. At this writing, no new developments have occurred.

In an attempt to "restore prayer to the public schools," an Al-abama legislator secured passage of a "moment of silence" law for his state's public schools. In the course of the debate on the bill the lawmaker admitted that the intent of the moment of silence was to encourage public school students to pray. When the moment of silence program was implemented in Mobile, Alabama, a parent, Ishmael Jafree, objected. Mr. Jafree declared himself to be an atheist and did not want his children subjected to religion in the public schools, even if only for a moment of silence. When he could not get relief from the school board, he filed a lawsuit in Judge Brevard Hand's federal district court.

In rendering his decision, the judge claimed to have uncovered some history that put the First Amendment in a new light. Judge Hand said that Thomas Jefferson was serving in France during the framing of the U.S. Constitution and the Bill of Rights. Since Mr. Jefferson was abroad and did not participate in the development of the Constitution, his 1802 "wall of separation" metaphor was an incorrect understanding of the Religion Clauses.

On the basis of that dubious rewriting of American history, Judge Hand declared the silent-prayer law constitutional. He went on to say that the Bill of Rights applied only to the federal government, that the Fourteenth Amendment could not bind the Bill of Rights on the states; therefore, if the State of Alabama wanted to establish its own religion, it had the right and the U.S. Supreme Court could not interfere.

In its 6-to-3 reversal, the U.S. Supreme Court expressed amazement at Hand's reasoning. Justice Sandra Day O'Connor stood with the "liberal" wing of the court in reversing the decision. She paid close attention to the legislative history of the Alabama law; that is, she examined what the legislature had done and said in the process of writing it. She concluded that the state legislature wanted to do more than simply have a moment of silence. The lawmakers, in fact, intended to circumvent the *Engel* case with their "moment of silence" law. She was not fooled for a moment.

In the *Jafree* case, the issue of secular humanism in the public schools received considerable attention. In the proceedings, Judge Hand let it be known that he would welcome a case examining the tenets of secular humanism. He did not have to wait long.

A group of parents, primarily from a conservative Baptist church in Mobile, obliged Hand and filed a lawsuit challenging a long list of textbooks used in the Mobile schools, saying that they taught the religion of secular humanism. In this legal round Pat Robertson's Legal Defense Fund paid the bill for the plaintiffs, the parents. People for the American Way paid the legal bills for the Mobile school board, which, incidentally, expressed great reluctance even to get involved in the hassle. Supposedly they would have allowed the parents to dictate curriculum rather than go to the trouble of another trial.

A lengthy trial, *Smith v. Mobile County Board of School Commissioners*, ensued. Expert witnesses for both sides testified. The tenets of the "religion" of secular humanism were examined. Witnesses for the school board denied that secular humanism was a religion. Witnesses for the parents alleged just the opposite.

In his ruling, Judge Hand decided that, indeed, secular humanism was a religion, that it was indeed being taught through the textbooks, that the teaching of secular humanism violated the "no establishment" clause, and that, on the basis of the separation of church and state, the textbooks should be forthwith removed. He issued an order banning forty-five State Selection Committee-approved textbooks from the schools. When the schools pleaded to let them finish the year with the books, the judge refused. The school board appealed to the Eleventh Circuit Court of Appeals in Atlanta, which stayed the judge's decision until the end of the school term.

Most established First Amendment organizations in the country objected to Judge Hand's ruling. Finding the angle to appeal his decision proved more difficult. The judge had turned the tables, using church/state separation as a means to remove the offensive textbooks. In some other cases, federal courts have felt compelled to define religion in order to determine the validity of the claims of religious groups who came before their bench, so Judge Hand had precedent in declaring secular humanism a religion.

What's more, the First Amendment groups had already reached the conclusions that social study textbooks had consistently, for decades, ignored the important place of religion in American history. They vigorously disagreed with the judge when he said the vacuum had been created because of the influence of secular humanists. Studies reveal that textbooks had ignored religion for many years but not out of a diabolical plot to remove religion from our history; rather, because publishers wanted to avoid controversy that might arise over conversations about religion.

The rulings by Judge Hull and Judge Hand have their positive and negative dimensions. They could create serious problems in public school education if parents can force the systems to create a cafeteria-style curriculum. In a complex society, curriculum should reflect its pluralism. However, the public puts the schools in an impossible bind if they expect all the views, and the shades of all the views, to be anticipated by the educational program. By the same token, public school planners make a fundamental mistake in community relations when they arrogantly disregard the religious and ethnic mix of their students. Ultimately, the public school administrators and teachers work for the public—the taxpayers—and must take the public's needs and wishes into account.

Publishers have to sell textbooks and make a profit, if they mean to stay in business. Controversy hurts sales and subjects school boards to protests and lawsuits. For a number of years, textbook publishers in an almost unconscious collusion with selection committees have "dumbed" down textbooks; that is, they have subtly removed potentially controversial material from their texts, especially in science, history, social studies, and health.

A rising tide of complaints from all quarters of the public has forced public school officials and textbook publishers to take a hard look at curriculum materials. Even though I object to the paranoid nitpicking of some of the ultra-conservative groups, they have played an important role in forcing decision-makers to reexamine texts and curriculum.

Several church/state angles arise:

No one religious group can be allowed to dictate school policy. Especially in smaller communities, the prevailing religious majority can exert pressure on school boards, attempting to force the authorities to lean in the direction of the more powerful religious group. School boards do well to listen to *all* groups, to take the varying points of view into account, then to make the fairest decisions possible.

In this connection, a disturbing two-pronged political problem involving school board elections has occurred in some communities. The first problem has come when people with a decidedly anti-public school bias manage to get themselves elected or chosen for public school boards. In one major city, the majority of seats on the school board were held by citizens whose children attended parochial schools. These private school parents effectively held public schools hostage. Essential programs were blocked. Bond issues for school construction were delayed, gutted, or blocked entirely. Sometimes these school board members seem to say, "If we cannot get money for our private schools, we will make life miserable for public school administrators and impede all the programs we can." Indeed, races for public school boards may well become a crucial battleground for maintaining the integrity of the nation's public schools.

The second problem has come when people with a decidedly fundamentalist religious view have managed to get on the school board. Their children attended public schools, but they have seemed to want to convert non-sectarian public schools into Bible academies. Science and social studies teachers face a steady barrage of criticism from the fundamentalist-dominated school boards.

These unfortunate configurations on public school boards occur most easily when the members of the board are elected from the community at large. Frequently, school board races draw little attention from the public. They are often held off-season, so they draw low voter turnout. Pressure groups of one kind or another delight in such elections because they are ready-made for takeover by a small, determined group. Citizens with strong commitments to public education must take greater notice of the people who run for school boards. We do not need any laws saying who can or cannot run for public office. We certainly do not want religious or, if you please, non-religious tests for office. The public gets the kind of government, at any level, that it wants. My word of caution—and it is a strong word—is that the community must take notice of who runs for the school board. When all is said and done, the board may have more direct bearing on the quality of life in a community and in the country as a whole than any other public officials.

Persons in positions to make policy decisions about textbooks should be encouraged to demand the highest quality possible. Avoid books that speak to the lowest common denominator in the society. If the question of a textbook turns on a church/state issue, the administrators should go for quality, thereby serving church and state much more adequately.

Over the next few years, social studies textbooks will begin to incorporate a more careful rendering of the role of religion in American history. While religious people will applaud this change, they should also be prepared to take the bitter with the sweet. American religion has had its dark moments. In the name of religion, Quakers were hanged in Boston, blacks beaten and lynched in the South, Mormons driven out of Illinois, Baptist preachers imprisoned in Virginia, and Jews and Catholics sometimes relegated to second-class citizenship. The whole story deserves telling for the sake of truth and scholarship. We need education, not propagandizing, about religion in our history.

At this writing, the clearest attempt to inject a religious doctrine into the public schools' curriculum comes from those who want creationism included in the public school science curriculum. Since Charles Darwin first introduced his primitive theories of evolution in the middle of the nineteenth century, many in the religious community, particulary those who hold a strict, literalist view of the Bible, have had rigors. It seems to make no difference that Darwin's theories have long ago been surpassed; some strict conservatives keep fighting the antievolution battles.

A school of thought has arisen called "creation science." Followers of this line of reasoning challenge theories of evolution from a number of angles, but with the bottom-line assertion that creation came into being at once by divine decree. Proponents go to great lengths to shoot holes in all the theories that hold out for a vast universe of undeterminable but ancient origin. Despite their efforts to create a science, the real basis for creationism is the biblical account of beginnings as found in the opening chapters of the Book of Genesis. The various theories of evolution, in the minds of biblical literalists, pose profound threats to the validity of the Bible. Attempts by public school science teachers to talk about the origins of the universe without giving direct reference to the biblical accounts throw parents with a strict creationist view into consternation. So the battle over theories of origins of the universe has raged for much of this century.

The famous Scopes Trial of 1925 in Dayton, Tennessee, drove the issue underground for fifty years. In the early 1980s fundamentalists persuaded the Arkansas state legislature to pass a bill requiring that creation science be taught along with the theory of evolution. United States District Judge William H. Overton ruled the Arkansas law unconstitutional (*McClain v. Arkansas Board of Education*), in violation of the "no establishment" clause of the First Amendment. The Arkansas school officials, who never had much of a stomach for the battle anyway, decided not to appeal the ruling.

On the heels of the Arkansas case, the Louisiana legislature passed a similar law. Both the federal district court and the Fifth Circuit Court of Appeals declared the law unconstitutional (*Edwards v. Aguilard*). Naturally the case went to the U.S. Supreme Court.

Religious liberty groups filed briefs in the case, asking the Supreme Court to uphold the lower courts' decisions declaring the law unconstitutional. These groups reasoned that creationism is essentially a religious doctrine taught by the Bible and other religious books. To require that creationism become part of the public school curriculum does indeed violate the "no establishment" clause of the First Amendment. The religious freedom groups went on to say that a teacher should be free to indicate that some religious groups do hold differing views on creation. Teachers who hold a variation on the creationist view certainly have the freedom to express their views. In fact, good pedagogy would suggest that all the views of creation be mentioned. But to require that creationism, a religious doctrine, be taught is poor public policy and poor religion.

In a seven to two decision, the High Court declared the Louisiana law unconstitutional because it violated the Establishment Clause of the First Amendment. The justices said that creationism clearly implied a creator, thus establishing the theological belief in some kind of God. The strong decision did not rule out discussions about various views of the origin of the earth. The decision simply says that as a religious doctrine, creationism could not be a required part of the public school curriculum. Creationists have vowed to keep up the fight, primarily by developing creation science textbooks and sneaking them into public schools through sympathetic teachers. Stay tuned. The issue will come up again.

Another educational question with implications for church/ state problems is values education in the public schools. We do not have the space to go into the involved debate about values education. Suffice it to say that steady outcries by people in every walk of life for more attention to values education in the public schools will bring about much debate and pronounced changes.

Whereas government, as government, should not try to promote religion in any way, particularly in the public schools, government does have a definite role to play in encouraging values that enhance the life of individuals and strengthen the state. Look at the Preamble to the U.S. Constitution. It is a list of values that *We The People* have covenanted to promote: justice, security in the world of nations, domestic tranquility, general welfare, and liberty both for today and for tomorrow.

But having agreed that government has a responsibility to promote basic values, we have to admit quickly that the task is not as easy as it sounds. We live in a country of almost bewildering pluralism. Values frequently compete with one another. Who will teach the values? What values will receive emphasis? Will the values of education occur in the context of existing courses such as social studies, home economics, and biology, or will the schools set up special classes that deal with values?

Preliminary efforts have created controversy. Discussions about Americans' responsibilities to care about the world's problems, especially hunger and population explosion, meet with resistance from those who fear we will sacrifice our national sovereignty in some kind of "one-world" government. Discussions about population control run into conflict with those who regard contraceptives and other methods of chemical birth control as murder of the unconceived.

Probably the most difficult problem facing those who advocate values education is the question of sex education. Some parents do not want sex education discussed at all in public schools. Others want the schools to take full responsibility for the problems of youthful sexual irresponsibility. What does a high school counselor do when a teenager asks advice about her unwanted pregnancy—especially when the young woman refuses to discuss her condition with her parents? Do the schools keep a supply of condoms in the principal's desk drawer to distribute to sexually active youth?

One day, a reporter from the *New York Times* called to get my reaction to the steadily rising debate over values education. I told the reporter I would have to look at the proposed list of values and investigate the teaching methods, but that, generally, I supported the concept.

"How can you reconcile the separation of church and state with the teaching of values," she queried.

I responded by saying that no one is advocating teaching a Bible lesson in values class. Western civilization has a reservoir of biblically symbol-oriented values that have contributed to our collective greatness. We can emphasize that pool of values without having to quote chapter and verse from the Bible. As a matter of fact, all the world's great civilizations say they believe in fairness, the Golden Rule, honesty, justice, sexual responsibility, etc. People generally at least give lip service to these broad tenets, regardless of the Holy Book they read.

I told the reporter that one can even discuss these values by referring to the Bible, if, out of fairness and in deference to the quality of their instruction, due notice was given to other great Holy Books also. The Bible does not have a monopoly on moral and ethical teachings.

We do not need to create a Department of Values. The debate, the conversation is productive. One of the most positive contributions that political and religious conservatives have made to public policy is their emphasis on "traditional values." If their somewhat narrow and humorless way of approaching the subject makes us uncomfortable, we must hear what they say and become involved in the debate for values education that emerges.

The content and methods for values education in the public schools demand careful monitoring. Strong political and religious forces would like to seize the debate and shape it in their own image. Since most of us live in the broad middle ground, we must not give way to extremists on the left or the right. People on the extreme left tend to say, "Do your own thing." People on the extreme right tend to say, "Do it my way, or else." Either extreme must be avoided if the nation's moral foundations are to remain strong.

Those of us committed to the separation of church and state have a role to play: if nothing else, to keep the debate from falling apart at the exact point of the separation of church and state. My colleagues and I have participated regularly in colloquia discussing values education. We believe the process can occur without infringing religious liberty and we intend to remain in the process in order to run interference for everyone's religious freedom.

Public education has always faced steady criticism from the community. The country has more than its share of "experts" who know exactly how to run a school system and have no hesitation in expressing their views to all who will listen. And certainly an enterprise as mammoth as the American public school system will have numerous weak links. Certainly, not every teacher can measure up to the ideal. Philosophies come and go, wax and wane, catch the public's eye, seem successful but then fall out of favor for a variety of reasons. An approach that seems perfectly logical this year may look absolutely ridiculous next time around. But we still have a great system of public education that needs and deserves our support as well as constructive criticism.

It appears that many citizens of the more ultra-conservative persuasion seem determined to destroy the public schools. The rhetoric that comes from the right side of the political spectrum about public schools quickly becomes vicious. One looks for constructive criticism in their comments, only to find it all but lacking.

Many in the country have allowed themselves to believe that the public school enterprise has come under the power of secular humanists, who are, in turn, out to turn the country into a people who are anti-God, anti-family, anti-country. Ridiculous. The country has become increasingly secular. Our traditional commitments to religion—even that of church with dinner afterwards at Mom's—have diminished, but not because of a conspiracy by a vicious corps of secular humanists. The changes come almost inexorably, but not irreversibly, with the passage of time. With great effort from large cross-sections of the people of the country we can manage changes, make recommitments to transcendent values, and move into the next century. Bashing away at basic institutions like the public schools system can only hasten the overall erosion of what we cherish most about the country. Rather than more great divorces in our country, we need new efforts at reconciliation.

Use of Public Property for Religious Purposes

In 1979, Pope John Paul II came to the United States for a grand tour. Everywhere he stopped, hundreds of thousands of people turned out to welcome him. Roman Catholics gathered in vast throngs in public places to participate in Papal Masses conducted by their spiritual leader. In asking what use can religious groups make of public property, the Pope's visit can provide some guidelines.

To prepare for his visit and the Mass he would conduct in Philadelphia, the city officials paid for and constructed a handsome worship stand in Logan Square. According to stories growing out of the episode, Cardinal Krol, Archbishop of Philadelphia, offered to pay for the altar but Mayor Frank Rizzo, in an effort to show the generosity of the city, overrode him and decided that the city would foot the bill.

When the press reported that the city had paid for the worship stand, great protests went up around the country, especially in Philadelphia. Citizens understood that the city would have a large financial outlay in providing security for the Pope, in handling traffic, and in moving the hundreds of thousands who would come to see this world figure. They may have groaned at the cost, but the city had a responsibility to provide such basic services for any duly certified public gathering. Nevertheless, tax money paying for a place to conduct public worship is quite another matter. Concerned Philadelphia taxpayers, along with Americans United for Separation of Church and State, sought and received legal remedy. The archdiocese of Philadelphia had to reimburse the city for the cost of the Papal Mass platform.

John Paul's tour also called for a visit to Washington, D.C., including a Mass on the Smithsonian Mall in the center of the city. The archdiocese requested permission from the city to use the mall for the Mass. Madalyn Murray O'Hair and a group of atheists objected to the use of the mall by religious groups for any purpose. They lodged a lawsuit to enjoin the Pope from using public property for religious purposes, saying that the use of the mall for the worship service violated the First Amendment. In this instance, Americans United for Separation of Church and State and other First Amendment organizations came to the defense of the Pope. As a bona fide member of the community, the archdiocese had every right to use the mall. Of course the city would provide security and other crowd control measures, but tax money would not be used to pay for worship or materials directly involved in worship. The archdiocese paid for the worship stand, a proper and constitutional action.

The cutting edge in these decisions is the role of government in supporting, promoting, or encouraging religion. Since government had no role in fostering religion in the Pope's visit to Washington, the Constitution did not suffer.

The most notable Supreme Court case that spoke to this issue arose out of a dispute in the city of Pawtucket, Rhode Island. For some years, the city council had provided a Christmas display in a small city park as part of the town's seasonal decorations. Since before anyone could remember otherwise, the council-sponsored display had included a Nativity Scene: a crèche depicting the baby Jesus in the manger with Mary and Joseph looking on.

Some people in town began to object to the presence of the city-owned, -maintained, and -displayed Nativity Scene. When the city council refused to remove the crèche from their decorations, the objectors—you guessed it—filed a lawsuit. Naturally the case went all the way to the U.S. Supreme Court, as *Lynch v. Donnelly.* To the dismay of church/state separationists, the High Court in a 5-to-4 decision upheld the right of the city to display the crèche. In applying his own Lemon test, Chief Justice Warren Burger, writing for the court, said that the Nativity Scene passed all three prongs: The Christmas display, including the crèche, had the secular effect of encouraging people to come to town and shop. The majority went on to say that the Nativity Scene had lost its religious symbolism and had, rather, simply become part of America's celebration of Christmas—which had also lost its religious significance.

The dissenting opinion from the Supreme Court displayed much more sensitivity. Justice William J. Brennan writing for the dissenters, said that, if the Nativity Scene meant anything at all, it was an important symbol of religious belief.

In the opinion of many legal experts in the church/state field, this decision muddies the waters in an unfortunate way. For the last forty years, the Supreme Court had been fairly consistent in upholding the Jeffersonian/Madisonian view of the separation of church and state, until this case. This decision leaves considerable confusion about the use of public property by religious groups, especially the government's role in supporting such use.

For twenty years, a Christian cross has perched atop its water tower in St. Cloud, Florida. It had stood there for so long the townspeople hardly noticed it, even at night, when it glowed with electric lights. Then someone moved to town who objected to the cross maintained on top of the water tower at taxpayers' expense. The newcomer began to make discreet inquiries of the city officials as to the why's and wherefore's of the cross. In no uncertain terms the newcomer was told to mind his business. According to the story, that person left town. But someone else, not a resident, made noises like he would bring a lawsuit seeking to have the cross removed from public property.

A radio-talk-show host in Orlando made keeping the cross in its place on the water tower a *cause célèbre*, kicking up quite a ruckus in the process. At this writing, the cross remains on its twenty-year perch.

In an appearance on that particular talk show, I was asked what I thought about the cross. At first, seeking to be diplomatic and avoid the hotseat, I tried to sound legal and constitutional. When the host pressed me, I had to say, "I do not think the cross should to be on the water tower. I do not think the city should pay for its maintenance."

"But the majority of the people in town have no problem with its presence on the water tower," the talk-show host insisted.

"I have no doubt about that. Probably a large majority do not object to the cross. Fortunately, constitutional questions do not require a voting majority to be upheld," I said.

If I could do that interview again, thanks to further research, I would quote Supreme Court Justice Robert H. Jackson in his opinion in *West Virginia State Board of Education v. Barnette* (1943), which overturned the repressive decision in the *Gobitis* case (the flag salute case involving Jehovah's Witnesses children). For the court, Justice Jackson declared:

> The very purpose of a Bill of Rights was to withdraw certain subjects from the vicissitudes of political controversy, to place them beyond the reach of majorities and officials and to establish them as legal principles to be applied to the courts. One's right to life, liberty, and property, to free speech, a free press, freedom of worship and assembly, and other fundamental rights may not be submitted to vote; they depend on the outcome of no elections.

A synagogue in Grand Rapids, Michigan, secured permission to place a menorah in Calder Plaza opposite City Hall for the season of Hanukkah. The synagogue agreed to maintain the symbol for the two weeks it would remain in place. The Grand Rapids chapter of Americans United for Separation of Church and State wrote the city council requesting that the menorah be removed because it violated the First Amendment, giving the impression that the city endorsed the religious faith represented by the symbol. In that instance, the separationist troops divided in friendly disagreement when the home office of the AU saw no problem with the synagogue's using city property for a limited time at their own expense.

As a carry-over from days gone by, many state and municipal seals include religious symbols, especially crosses. To the credit of the local governments, when well-meaning local citizens have objected to the use of the religious symbols in official city seals, the religious symbols have been quietly replaced with more secular representations. Even though such instances would not be of sufficient importance to attract a national group to lodge a lawsuit, I applaud the sensitivity of the local authorities in reflecting the changing times. The cause of religion is not advanced by such symbolism, nor is it impeded by their removal. Certainly, community harmony is advanced by their removal once serious objections are voiced.

At this writing, several cities in the United States are feverishly preparing for another tour by Pope John Paul II in the fall of 1987. He will visit Miami, which has a large Roman Catholic population. Over protests from the teacher organization and the calendar-planning committee, the Dade County School Board has acceded to a request from the Archbishop of Miami by giving all the students a holiday on the day the Pope celebrates Mass in Tamiami Stadium. President Reagan is scheduled to greet the Pope the day before the Mass. The school board did not grant a holiday for the joint meeting of the President and the Pope, just the day of the Papal Mass. The board cited problems of traffic.

At least one member of the school board and several religious leaders objected to the granting of the school holiday.

The American Civil Liberties Union considered a legal protest, but then decided not to get into a hassle over the holiday. Americans United for the Separation of Church and State has officially protested the holiday. If the board does not rescind its action, AU will consider a lawsuit citing violation of the "no establishment" clause and using the Lemon test as cause for the action.

In its letter to the Dade County School Board, Americans United agreed that the Pope is a world figure for whom many students in Dade County have special affection. The school board could easily give excused absences to all students who wanted to attend the Mass without violating the rights of other non-Catholic students, who would better spend their day in class. Besides, if the city felt anxious about traffic problems, to loose more than 250,000 students on the city—most of whom would *not* attend the mass—would only add to the congestion.

The bottom line: Government cannot support or encourage religion without violating the First Amendment. The "free exercise" of religion of the Catholic students who wish to attend the Papal Mass can easily be accommodated short of the school board's violation of the "no establishment of religion" clause.

Many churches, especially those in suburban areas, began their institutional life meeting in public school buildings on Sundays. Is that a violation of the separation of church and state? Not if all religious groups have equal access to the public's property and if all groups pay the same rent for use of the building.

What about those groups that stand in airline terminals and pass out their literature inviting the public to become inquirers into their religion? In most cases, the courts have allowed the religious groups to witness in public places as long as they do not seek to interfere with traffic flow.

The bottom line: Religious groups should have ready access to public property in keeping with good public policy and fair play. Government should not fund the activities or symbols, other than minimal maintenance for safety's sake and/or fire and police protection.

Military, Prison, and Congressional Chaplains

Should the taxpayers of the nation pay salaries and expenses of men and women to serve as chaplains to the military forces, in prisons, and to legislative bodies? We have to examine the three broad categories.

Military Chaplains. The military chaplaincy began in 1775 when the Continental Congress provided funds to pay for chaplains. The following year, the Congress authorized the appointment of ordained ministers to serve as chaplains. George Washington implemented the congressional decision, thus receiving credit for being the father of the military chaplaincy.

The chaplaincy has had its own evolution. In 1823, the practice of requiring that chaplains be ordained and accredited by an identifiable religion became official. In 1838, the practice of having post chaplains became firmly entrenched by regulation. President Polk appointed the first Catholic chaplain in 1846. In 1861, President Lincoln requested that a Jewish chaplain be appointed.

In 1854, in the context of a drive to get rid of congressional chaplains, objectors made a run at the military chaplaincy too. Their efforts to have chaplains removed from the federal payroll failed. Part of the rationale for military chaplains paid for by the government is that people serving in the armed services do not have access to religious worship as do civilians. "Free exercise" of religion for military personnel outweighs the danger to the "no establishment" clause.

Prison Chaplains. American religious institutions have paid close attention to prisons. Early in our history, the various churches provided chaplains to some prisons out of concern for the spiritual welfare of the inmates and as part of a larger, ongoing program of prison reform. Generally, both federal and state prisons provide chaplaincy services.

The courts have generally held that inmates cannot be forced to attend worship services within the prison. In a few cases, Protestant and Roman Catholic chapels are on prison grounds, but generally, and more appropriately, a common facility is provided for worship services.

The proliferation of religious groups in the country is matched within prison walls. Native American religion, Black Muslims, satan worshipers, and many more sects constantly clamor for recognition and an opportunity to practice their religion within penal institutions, thus causing ongoing debates between inmates and prison administrators.

At this writing, serious challenges to the constitutionality of prison chaplains are not taking place. While a church/state separation purist might question the practice on technical grounds, prison chaplains are not being questioned.

Congressional Chaplains. In 1774, the Continental Congress appointed Reverend Jacob Duche to serve as chaplain. Shortly after his election, Reverend Duche advocated that General Washington abandon the war and abrogate the Declaration of Independence, providing a rather unfortunate beginning to the office of Congressional Chaplain. Others who came after him, however, had impeccable credentials as patriots. The First Congress established under the U.S. Constitution continued the practice of having a chaplain open the daily sessions with prayer.

When Benjamin Franklin suggested spoken prayers during the sessions of the Constitutional Convention in the summer of 1787, his fellow delegates did not go along. They expressed no hostility toward religion, but the move did not suit the temper of the meetings and, in the view of some delegates, could have further muddied the political waters.

The practice of having congressional chaplains continues to this day. For most of our history, the chaplains served only in a part-time capacity. Beginning in 1979, the House of Representatives employed a full-time chaplain, providing a salary commensurate with one in such a position. The Senate soon followed suit.

Of all the chaplaincy institutions, I find this one the most troubling from a constitutional point of view, although I hold in high regard both gentlemen who, at this writing, occupy the positions. They provide valuable service to the Congress as counselor in times of stress. They oversee funeral arrangements when a member of Congress dies. I have no quarrel with their service. I do question the taxpayer's paying their salaries. The question, however, is moot because the U.S. Supreme Court has upheld the constitutionality of congressional and legislative chaplains. Of all the battles that clamor for attention, we will not soon turn to this one.

Tax Exemption for Church Property

The Emperor Constantine (A.D. 280–337), as part of his conversion from paganism to Christianity, granted tax exemption to churches and to the property close around them used for sacred activities. From the earliest days of colonial history, churches enjoyed an exemption from property taxes. Most Americans accept such exemptions as part of our way of life and only rarely do vigorous challenges to this privilege arise. State and federal law have extended church property tax exemption on the grounds that churches and other benevolent institutions serve the public good. Tax exemption is a way of recognizing and encouraging public service by servant institutions.

Through the years, voices from within the religious community have decried the practice, saying the church should be completely free from obligation to the state. Some First Amendment groups point out, correctly, that the exemption is at least indirect aid to the church.

Churches should understand that tax exemption does not exist as a right but as a privilege. Freedom to conduct their worship without government interference does not necessarily entail tax exemption. In our own day, as some churches become increasingly active politically, they create the possibility that the public will begin demanding revocation of property tax-exempt status. All over the country, money-starved municipalities that live on property taxes have begun to limit the amount and kind of land and buildings that can remain tax exempt. A long court battle ended in Texas when the judge ruled that indeed the county tax assessor could enter a church campground on the tax rolls. As an accommodation, the assessor and the church group came to an agreement to pay at a lower rate. But pay taxes they do.

Another church bought a piece of property next to its facilities to hold for future expansion. They made no use of the valuable lot for church purposes. The green eyes of the city tax assessor fell on the ground and levied taxes that the church had to pay. Long ago, the courts ruled that government could levy both property and income taxes on businesses owned by churches and religious orders.

The strongest argument for continued tax exemption is the opportunity for government to become excessively entangled in church affairs by levying taxes. Religious ministries should not face hassle by the tax assessor. The threat of taxation must never become a tool for repression in the hands of unfriendly government officials. In some instances religious groups have taken the commendable action of voluntarily giving the local municipality money to help offset the costs of city services such as fire and police protection.

Benign Symbols:
The Motto and Pledge to the Flag

In God We Trust. During the Civil War, the U.S. government in the person of the Secretary of the Treasury, reflecting a concern in the country that the United States give more public attention to God, ordered that the phrase *"In God We Trust"* be inscribed on some coins. In 1864, the phrase began appearing on U.S. coinage; in 1865, the Congress retroactively approved the move.[8]

President Theodore Roosevelt, in his day, objected to the phrase being placed on coins, and stopped the procedure. The President felt that placing such a lofty phrase on money cheapened the meaning of the phrase. In 1908, the Congress ordered the phrase restored to coins—and there it has remained.[9] In 1955, during the Eisenhower "moral revival," "In God We Trust" became the official motto of the United States.

Certainly the motto reflects the conviction of most Americans, if one puts any stock in public polls. It certainly does no harm, while one could wonder if it does any good. I know of no serious effort to have the motto changed. Nor would it go anywhere in Congress if such a move were to be made.

"God" in the Pledge of Allegiance. President Eisenhower heard a sermon one Sunday at his church in which the minister suggested that the pledge to the flag could be strengthened if a "definitive factor in the American way of life" were added. Within three days, Senator Homer Ferguson of Michigan introduced a resolution adding the phrase "one nation *under God*" to the pledge of allegiance. By May 1954, the new pledge of allegiance became law.

Senator Ferguson wrote an opinion that the pledge did not violate the First Amendment, and there the matter has remained. Again, no First Amendment group has made a serious effort to have "under God" removed from the pledge.

In my view, these benign breakdowns of the separation of church and state are so minimal in their impact that they do not warrant full-scale challenges. They have no secular purpose, they fail the Lemon test, but so be it. With President Theodore Roosevelt, I agree that inclusion of the name of God in the pledge of allegiance and on our coins "comes close to sacrilege." I have an idea that Amos, Jeremiah, and a few other of the Old Testament prophets would give us Americans a hard time for misusing the Divine Name. But we will leave that fight for another day.

Overarching Dangers to Church and State

We have described only some of the problems we face in church/state relations today. We can deal with the problems. But, running through the problems, some subtle but real dangers threaten religious freedom and, with it, pose threats to all our freedoms.

We face the danger of a stifling kind of conformity for the sake of order. One has only to read the daily newspapers to know that American society is bucking and heaving like the untamed mustang of the Wild West. Our problems of disorder and instability present themselves in such living color on every hand that they need no cataloging. Suffice it to say that all of us must work diligently to manage our tumultuous society.

In such a social climate people come along genuinely concerned about our future and set about to find ways to impose order on our people. One of the key ways such order has come in the past is to bring all the people under one religion. Indeed, one of the reasons most countries have maintained an established religion has been to keep the people's passions—religious and political—under control. In the process of attempting to make all people dot the same i's and cross the same t's religiously, a stifling conformity has frequently settled on a people.

I view the efforts by some on the extreme right side of the national spectrum to have state-required prayer and Bible reading in the public schools as an effort to bring about social stability through religious conformity. While I am for national order and homogeneity, we must not attempt to achieve it by trying to squeeze the American people into one religious mold. In the first place, it will not work. In the second place, such efforts will bring about deep divisions in the country. But the efforts persist.

I also get the uneasy feeling that some business moguls who pour money into ultra-conservative political/religious campaigns do so not out of concern for the spiritual welfare of the American people. Instead, religion can contribute to a more orderly society, and an orderly society is good for business. Make everyone behave and they will buy more beer or clothes or insurance.

A nation like ours, with something like two thousand religious groups competing for the attention of the people, lives on the edge of bigotry, hatred, and fear. We look with horror on the Holocaust of World War II. We say, "That can never happen here."

Says who? Of course it can happen here. We have super-manipulators in our society who have mastered the fine art of stirring up hatred and suspicions. We are only just now freeing ourselves from prejudice against black people. New religions come along that look and sound different. Establishment groups go to work on the "new boy on the block," without bothering to find out what "he" really believes. All kinds of conspiracies get hatched out. The latest is the "secular humanist" conspiracy. If you do not agree with your neighbor's political views, smear her with a secular humanist label. Americans have done that kind of smearing before against Jews, Roman Catholics, Orientals, Indians, etc. No, do not say we cannot have an American

Holocaust. We can. With religion's power to bless as well as curse, any civilization faces the danger of unleashing its own form of inquisition.

Some of the religious/political action groups have engaged in a form of religious terrorism against opponents. In 1980, John Buchanan, a nine-term veteran Alabama Republican, lost his party's nominating primary in large part because of religious terrorism. He had cast votes in some rather exotic legislation that Moral Majority types used to label him as anti-American, anti-family. For instance, he had voted for Panama Canal Treaty Implementation legislation that, simply, provided funds for the treaty the Senate had ratified. Since the House of Representatives, in which he served, has nothing to do with treaty ratification, he could in no way be accused of "giving away the Panama Canal." Moral Majority opponents put out the word that Buchanan was anti-American, not for a strong defense, and soft on Communism because he had cast his vote in a way they did not approve. The Moral Majority purported to be the party of Christian values. Religious terrorism.

Senators who voted for a bill containing some funding for family-planning organizations found themselves labeled "baby killers" by religious anti-abortion groups. In the convoluted reasoning of some religiously oriented political action groups, a vote for the Department of Education earned the label "anti-family." Men and women who enter the political lists expect to hear bad news from their opponents. How unfortunate for church and state when religious groups toss around those distortions. Religious terrorism.

When Americans United for Separation of Church and State quoted Pat Robertson from one of his television broadcasts and ran his statements in its publication, he threatened lawsuits of libel. When the organization quoted his quotes, he backed away. Religious terrorism.

In the course of all this squabbling and labeling, legitimate struggles for moral consensus get lost in sectarian infighting. Profound human needs get shunted aside in these political/religious maneuverings.

Then a subtle but fierce danger arises. When religious groups fall out with each other and begin an inordinate amount of fighting, the state moves in to become the protector of religion, then the supporter; the arbiter, then the user of religion. Canny politicians are always ready to seize on the energies of religion and use them for their own purposes. In this deteriorating climate, the vitality of the Republic and the religious community are blunted, then lost. We must not let that happen.

CHAPTER FOURTEEN

The Vision

What did the Founders envision for America's religious community? What did they hope to achieve through the First Amendment? How did they see the principle of the separation of church and state working itself out in American society?

The Founders envisioned a vital religious community struggling to meet human spiritual, emotional, and physical needs. They envisioned a religious community speaking to, quarreling with, praying for, but not becoming coincidental with any government. They envisioned a political life informed by, reacting with, appreciative of, but separate from the institutions of religion. Those who created our nation envisioned revealed religion maintaining its distinctions, but with its public, patriotic extensions becoming part of the moral lifeline of the nation.

The Founders' dream must be reinterpreted, translated in every generation. How? Let me conclude by offering some broad suggestions about how both church and state can realize the Founders' dream of religious liberty for all Americans. (I am indebted to Dr. James E. Wood, Jr., of Baylor University, for this framework.)[1] The application of religiously based principles in politics must be made by people with political competence. If one wants to address the question of labor, he must know something about labor relations; if education, she must know something about education. No substitute exists for political literacy, which includes knowing something about government and the Constitution. Being a religious person gives one no more competence in politics than in art, music, law, or medicine.

Do I advocate political elitism? Can only those with political science degrees take part in politics? Of course not. But our country is best served when we the people pay the price to gain some knowledge of the way the system actually works. It is appalling how little so many people know about our basic system. Frequently, men and women who know their own jobs well cannot tell the difference between a senator and a representative. When asked to name some of the members of the national cabinet, they falter. When quizzed on the particulars of a political view they espouse, they stumble. Indeed, political illiteracy abounds in this land of the free. Our collective life depends on the proper working of the political process. People who seek to make a statement of their religious perspective in politics have a special responsibility to become politically literate.

In my travels, I regularly encounter people who pick up all their news from one source. All too often they listen primarily to one commentator, or read only one paper or magazine. Citizens must pay the price to read and listen more widely. Only then can we make the most intelligent decisions, and even then it can be extremely difficult to find accuracy and truth.

Fortunately, even the illiterate can vote in America these days. But, to make a difference, we the people must pay the price to develop an ever-increasing measure of political competence. Political bumbling and ignorance make one prey to political operators who are all too ready to take advantage of our not-knowing.

The religious person must distinguish between moral imperatives and their particular applications to the body politic. Most Holy Books and world religions to which Americans give allegiance denounce injustice, racism, sexism, dishonesty, greed, super-nationalism, etc. But applying these grand, common principles to specific legislation and issues of public policy is not so easy. The Bible provides no blueprint for the ordering of society. The Bible was written in an era when people lived under despotic kings with no concept of democracy. Life was cheap; justice was quick, and often capricious. All the time, I encounter people who say, "Just apply the Bible to politics and we will get this country straightened out." Great. Which part of the Bible? Do we just pick up the Ten Commandments and place them over the Constitution? What if the two do not fit so snugly?

We proclaim justice. How do religious people translate justice into the everyday world? When an industrial plant begins to lose money, it faces the choices of staying open and going under, closing the plant, or relocating. In any event, people lose their jobs, which seriously undermines their way of life. Where is justice in a complicated situation like that? Indeed, it is not easy to apply the principle. It exacts no great price, requires no serious thinking to stand in a pulpit or before a television camera and decry injustice. It is quite another matter to get the grand principle translated into law and public policy.

How do we measure the effectiveness of a politician in expanding justice in a world all too often devoid of that precious commodity? How do we reconcile competing perspective on what is justice in a given situation?

Religious people must avoid absolutizing detailed applications of their religious beliefs and denouncing their political adversaries as being less religious or less righteous. I get terribly uncomfortable when people begin telling me *the* Christian point of view on any political issue. I take delight in discussing conflicting views of church and state issues with others provided they allow me to state my side without impugning my patriotism or religious convictions. Constructive debate and workable solutions to problems demand that people of goodwill be allowed to disagree.

Some of the nation's leading political leaders profess deep religious faith, yet they differ profoundly on the specifics of public policy and legislation. Fortunately, most of them have the wisdom not to label a brother or sister in the faith as unbelievers because they cannot agree on how much money to spend on an aircraft carrier, SDI, or Medicare. Would that more of their followers out in the hinterland had that same measure of grace.

Religious people involved in the political process must not make political issues into moral absolutes and moral absolutes into political issues.

Religious people must avoid the temptation to use political means for the accomplishment of religious ends—no less so than the temptation of politicians to use religion for the accomplishments of political ends.

The issues of school prayer and Bible reading in the public schools provide a case in point. People of religious faith, especially Christians, have a mandate to convert all people to their religion. Religious people believe that it is a good thing for all people to be religious, often just like themselves. Most Americans would agree that a balanced religious faith provides stability and good mental health to an individual. These are religious goals.

How does a particular group of religious people achieve that goal? In recent years, many have turned to government. Churches seem unable to reach young people in large numbers in order to pass on to them their faith perspective. Homes are under such stress; all too often their best energies are expended in just surviving. Little time is devoted to religious instruction. In the minds of many people, that leaves only the public schools. Evangelism, or conversion to religious faith, is not part of the curriculum of public schools. We should avoid asking government to do the job of religion.

From time immemorial, political leaders have sought to harness religious energies for their own political goals. We have seen this cynical, unscrupulous tactic used with skill in recent political campaigns. Candidates and politicians who have given little evidence of religious commitment have reached out to the vast throng of religious people, especially evangelicals, as a means to greater political power. Unfortunately, many of these believers have allowed themselves to be used by the politicians.

Religious people must ever be vigilant in recognizing the unholy alliance between any brand of religion and any brand of politics. To identify any nation with God, let alone any one political party, is to distort the prophetic role of religion and to deny the fundamental basis of a free and democratic society by making an idol of the state.

God does not belong to the United States. God is neither a Democrat nor a Republican. The healthiness of the political process suffers when one political party attempts to speak for God. The Constitution provides for a republic, not a theocracy.

The spirit of America calls for freedom, not simply toleration toward those with differing points of view. Toleration suggests that one view is *the* view while all others are borne as part of the burden for governance and power. By contrast, the U.S. Constitution ensures religious freedom, thus giving everyone equal standing before the law.

Religious freedom requires that the religious community carry its own weight, police itself. The religious should not look to government for moral and financial support. Religion should keep its own house in order, especially in matters of morals and doctrines, and it should avoid asking the "civil magistrate" to intervene.

The church/state vision for the rest of this century would include congregations' and other non-governmental groups' really getting serious about moral education, strengthening families, equipping Americans to deal effectively with the stresses of modern life. Religious groups can certainly interact with governmental entities in these kinds of efforts, while scrupulously maintaining their own independence.

The vision has to include concerted efforts for disparate religious groups to work together. My contact with most Americans, even those with whom I have deep political and constitutional differences, teaches me they generally want the same kind of country and religious community I want. We simply have to find ways to talk and work together. Labeling, perhaps unavoidable for purposes of discussion, has to be minimized. We have to lower our voices. If we ever intend to be the "City on the Hill" that our Pilgrim Fathers envisioned, we must come together, finding ways to reconcile differences or at least make them secondary to larger goals.

I hope that this book will contribute to the strengthening of religious liberty and provide a much clearer understanding of its indispensable friend and guarantor, the separation of church and state.

Notes

Chapter One
1. *Religion in America, 1986* (Princeton: Princeton Religious Research Center, October 1987). Forty percent of Americans tell the Gallup Poll they attended last church last Sunday. The figures probably are considerably lower, but are still above most Western nations.
2. James E. Wood, Jr., "Religious Fundamentalism and the Public Schools," *Journal of Church and State,* Vol. 29 (Winter 1987), p. 7.
3. Jim Castelli, *Pat Robertson: Extremist* (Washington, D.C.: People for the American Way, 1986).
4. William H. Marnell, *The First Amendment* (New York: Doubleday, 1964), p. xii.

Chapter Two
1. J. Gordon Milton, *The Encyclopedia of American Religion* (Wilmington, NC: McGrath, 1978).

Chapter Three
1. TCA 2-10-101 *et seq.*
2. Jim Buie, "We Are Mothers, Not Martyrs," *Church & State,* Vol. 36 (November 1983), pp 4–5.
3. *Religious Freedom Reporter,* Vol. 6 (April 1986), pp. 128–131.
4. *Church and State,* Vol. 39 (July–August 1987), p. 16.
5. *Religious Freedom Reporter,* Vol. 7 (January–February 1987), pp. 8–11.

Chapter Four

1. Nathan Schachner, *Thomas Jefferson: A Biography* (New York: Appleton-Century-Crofts, 1951), Vol. 2, p. 701.
2. "Roger Williams: Prophet of Freedom" *Church & State*, Vol. 28 (June 1975), pp. 4–5.
3. Schachner, p. 701.
4. *Writings of Thomas Jefferson*, Monticello Edition, Vol. 16, pp. 281–82.
5. Anson Phelps Stokes and Leo Pfeffer, *Church and State in the United States* (New York: Harper and Row, 1967), p. 55.
6. *Ibid.*, p. 53.
7. Thomas J. Curry, *The First Freedom* (New York: Oxford University Press, 1986), p. 222.
8. *Ibid.*, p. 140.
9. William Lee Miller, from a speech delivered in Alexandria, Virginia, September 30, 1986.
10. Curry, p. 146.
11. Norman Cousins, *In God We Trust* (New York: Harper and Row, 1958), p. 314.
12. *Ibid.*, p. 10.
13. Curry, p. 142.
14. Benjamin Franklin: Quote from "Should Tax Dollars Finance Parochial Schools?" in a brochure published by Americans United for Separation of Church and State, Silver Spring, Maryland.
15. Cousins, p. 49.
16. *Ibid.*, p. 48.
17. *Ibid.*, p. 60.
18. *Ibid.*, p. 61.
19. *Ibid.*, p. 74.
20. *Ibid.*, p. 74.
21. *Ibid.*, p. 94.
22. *Ibid.*, p. 95.
23. *Ibid.*, p. 295.
24. *Ibid.*, p. 297.
25. *Ibid.*, p. 320.
26. *Ibid.*, p. 324.

Chapter Five

1. Henry Kamen, *The Rise of Toleration* (New York: McGraw-Hill, 1967), p. 13.

Chapter Six

1. Thomas J. Curry, *The First Freedoms* (New York: Oxford University Press, 1986), p. 135.
2. Anson Phelps Stokes, *Church and State in the United States* (New York: Harper and Brothers, 1950), p. 194.
3. Winthrop S. Hudson, *Religion in America* (New York: Charles Scribner's Sons, 1981), p. 44.
4. Albert J. Menendez, *Classics of Religious Liberty* (Silver Spring, MD: Americans United Research Foundation, 1978), pp. 1–3.
5. Hudson, p. 31.
6. William H. Marnell, *The First Amendment* (New York: Doubleday, 1964), p. 75.

Chapter Seven

1. Thomas J. Curry, *The First Freedoms* (New York: Oxford University Press, 1986), p. 160.
2. Catherine Drinker Brown, *Miracle at Philadelphia* (Boston: Little, Brown, 1966), p. 214.
3. Albert J. Menendez, *No Religious Test* (Silver Spring, MD: Americans United for Separation of Church and State, 1987), p. 5.
4. *Ibid.*, p. 3.
5. Bowen, p. 217.
6. Menendez, *No Religious Test*, p. 15.
7. Bowen, p. 255.
8. Curry, p. 193.
9. Anson Phelps Stokes, *Church and State in the United States* (New York: Harper and Brothers, 1950), Vol. 1, p. 540.
10. James P. Reichley, *Religion in American Public Life* (Washington, DC: Brookings Institution, 1985).
11. Curry, p. 222.
12. *Ibid.*, p. 222.

Chapter Eight

1. Anson Phelps Stokes, *Church and State in the United States* (New York: Harper and Brothers, 1950), Vol. 1, p. 690.
2. *Ibid.*, p. 858.
3. Hudson, p. 215.
4. Stokes, p. 576.
5. William H. Marnell, *The First Amendment* (New York: Doubleday, 1964), p. 132.

Chapter Ten

1. Robert Michaelson, *Piety in the Public Schools* (New York: Macmillan, 1970), p. 5.
2. Anson Phelps Stokes and Leo Pfeffer, *Church and State in the United States* (New York: Harper and Row, 1967), p. 272.
3. Charles C. Haynes, *Religious Liberty in America: A Teacher's Resource Guide* (Silver Spring, MD: Americans United Research Foundation, 1986).
4. Peter Bracher, *et al.*, *Public Education Religion Studies: Questions and Answers* (Dayton, OH: Wright State University, 1974).

Chapter Eleven

1. William H. Marnell, *The First Amendment* (New York: Doubleday, 1964), p. 157.
2. R. B. Dierfield, *Religion and Public Education* (Washington, D.C.: Public Affairs Press, 1962).
3. Anson Phelps Stokes and Leo Pfeffer, *Church and State in the United States* (New York: Harper and Row, 1967), p. 125.

Chapter Thirteen

1. From various publications prepared by the New York Chapter of Public Education and Religious Liberty.
2. T. S. Eliot, *Murder in the Cathedral.*
3. Monroe Billington, "President Lyndon Johnson and the Separation of Church and State," *Journal of Church and State* (Winter 1987), p. 105.
4. *Amicus Curiae* Brief, *American Baptist Churches v. Reagan.*
5. Albert J. Menendez, unpublished article "Churches and Politics: Some Guidelines."
6. Jeffrey Hadden, *The Gathering Storm in the Churches* (New York: Doubleday, 1969).
7. John C. Bennett, *Christians and the State* (New York: Charles Scribner's Sons, 1958), p. 207.
8. Anson Phelps Stokes and Leo Pfeffer, *Church and State in the United States* (New York: Harper and Row, 1967).
9. *Ibid.*, p. 570.

Chapter Fourteen

1. From notes in a panel discussion by James E. Wood, Jr., Baylor University, Waco, TX, January 1985.